Is That You, God?

GOD?

True Stories from Everyday Life

Jane Perkins

ISBN: 978-1-4497-2733-8 (sc)
ISBN: 978-1-4497-2735-2 (e)
ISBN: 978-1-4497-2734-5 (hbk)
Library of Congress Control Number: 2011917267

WestBow Press books may be ordered through booksellers or by contacting:

WestBow Press
A Division of Thomas Nelson
1663 Liberty Drive
Bloomington, IN 47403
www.westbowpress.com
1-(866) 928-1240

Photographs © John Perkins and Jane Perkins
Book and cover design by John Perkins

All Scripture quotations, unless otherwise indicated, are taken from the Life Application Study Bible, NIV

Printed in the United States of America
WestBow Press rev. date: 2/13/2012

WestBow
PRESS
A DIVISION OF THOMAS NELSON

*Dedicated to those whose stories I
share and to my supportive family
and friends, but foremost to God.
I am forever grateful.*

CONTENTS

INTRODUCTION

Time and time again, I found myself being connected with extraordinary people from all walks of life. Most were complete strangers to me. Their presence in my life proved to be much more than coincidental.

Our meetings happened almost anywhere—from a second-floor hospital room to the checkout lane of a grocery, from a nursing home or personal care facility to a crowded sports center or buffet-style restaurant, and even beside the worn-out truck of a homeless family. Sometimes the person lived within my community but most often resided miles away. One actually claimed a homeland across the ocean.

Yet, in spite of many differences, a common thread connected our lives. I didn't choose these people; God did. I only chose to respond to my heart tugs, the promptings of the Holy Spirit—even when I didn't understand the *why*—which allowed our paths to cross in incredible ways.

Regardless of whether the person had lived a life of integrity or had spent time in prison, or whether young or elderly, each became my friend. Their trials and hardships affected my life. Their happiness and well-being became important to me, and nothing brought me greater joy than knowing they placed their faith and trust in Jesus.

Many of these people whose stories I share go unnoticed in today's society and have little or no voice. This book is their witness and mine. We thank God and give Him the glory for the amazing way He connected us in love and friendship and for His message of hope within each story.

As you read the following pages, I invite you to open your heart and to answer for yourself: *Is that You, God?*

CHAPTER ONE

A Mum and a Mission

Hearing God's call to deliver a mum to a complete stranger changed my life forever.

It was an unseasonably warm morning for February, and I found myself working in the yard in anticipation of spring. But in spite of the beautiful weather, I continued to be disappointed and discouraged by the possibility of not being able to have a child. Instead of allowing this circumstance to continually steal my joy, I stopped for a moment, turning my thoughts to God. I asked that He fill this void in my life with something meaningful.

That very morning, I felt a tug at my heart telling me to take a mum to a particular elderly lady, the one adopted by the women's circle at our church. I thought to myself, *Do what?* Because I was not a member of that group, I had no idea who this lady was or where she lived. I questioned, *God, why me?*

My first reaction was to ignore these thoughts and return to my yard work. Then I remembered the brightly colored mum I'd bought the previous day for no apparent reason. I could take the mum to this lady, but I would need more information about her.

I immediately phoned the president of the women's group. After learning their adopted friend, Mrs. Dickson, was a resident of a nearby nursing home, I placed the mum in my car and headed for the facility.

When I checked with the nurses' station, a staff member

Even though I knew little about Mrs. Dickson, it was obvious she had accepted Jesus in her heart. Her faith was real. As she called out for Jesus to come, I sensed her spiritual longing to be rid of her pain and to meet Jesus face-to-face as promised in the Bible: "Do not let your hearts be troubled. Trust in God; trust also in me. In my Father's house are many rooms; if it were not so, I would have told you. I am going there to prepare a place for you. And if I go and prepare a place for you, I will come back and take you to be with me that you also may be where I am" (John 14:1–3).

Mrs. Dickson already knew the location of her new home. She was ready to make the move.

The next morning, she met Jesus.

~~~

Because of our new bond of friendship, I visited with Genie at the funeral home before his mother's service. I left with a heavy heart. Even though we lived only twenty miles apart in adjacent counties, I doubted if we would ever see each other again.

Some five weeks later—I didn't know why—I felt an overwhelming sense of urgency to check on him. Without any contact information, I returned at once to the nursing home where his mother had been a patient. I asked the staff if they could give me his address or phone number without violating their privacy policy.

A nurse looked quite surprised and called my request "a strange coincidence," for Genie had just walked in the door a few minutes earlier to pick up his mom's belongings. As I met up with him in the hallway, we again recognized something greater than coincidence—God's perfect timing.

~~~

The day we first met, Genie and I were both hurting and cried out to God for help—Genie from his mom's hospital room and I from my backyard. Genie's heartache was about losing his mom and lifetime companion; mine was about longing to have a child. Accepting the possibility of not having children wasn't easy. But on that particular morning, feeling the need to move on with life, I had asked God to exchange that heartache for something meaningful.

Genie needed someone to comfort him; I needed someone to comfort. The way I look at it, we must have been a match in God's eyes, so He sent the Holy Spirit to connect us. Genie agrees, and we thank God and give Him the glory. God answered each of our prayers, and a lifetime of friendship began with a tug at my heart, a mum, and a mission.

because he has no air-conditioning or way to open windows for cross ventilation, the sun's hot rays beating down on his metal roof cause an unbearable heat buildup.

One day, when the humidity was extremely high and the temperature soared to nearly three digits, I became worried about Genie. I called to ask if he were keeping cool enough.

"Oh, yes," he responded.

"Are you using your fan?"

"No, not using a fan," he said with a chuckle. "I'm sitting under a shade tree, getting that . . . free breeze." The heat didn't spoil his sense of humor!

At times, when Genie had no means of transportation, he walked miles to church, the grocery, or wherever he needed to go. Occasionally, though, someone would notice and stop to give him a lift. He recently inherited a truck from a friend, the same truck he had used to drive his friend to and from cancer treatments. Although this truck usually proved dependable, it sometimes sat idle beside an old shade tree while Genie saved money to pay costly repair bills.

Genie's exposure to the outside world is limited. He seldom leaves home or socializes. A television was not a household item until recent years, and repairs became too costly to keep it operating. While the radio and newspaper are his main sources of receiving information, his used guitar is the means through which he shares his heart.

His guitar, what a blessing it has been! That instrument was given to him while working as a farmhand. Although he can't read music, he learned to play by ear. After strumming around on his guitar, he found that notes soon became tunes, and music became his life. Genie experienced some of his happiest moments while singing and playing bluegrass and gospel music.

Once he spent over a year teaching himself the notes and lyrics to more than twenty songs. After he learned how to sing them in two parts, he recorded his music on a tape. Even though he had no way to reproduce it for himself, he gave me his only copy. Receiving that tape left me thinking—*What a gift, having only one of something you dearly treasure and selflessly giving it away.*

Listening to his tape blessed my life, for Genie sang from his heart. One song, in particular, became most special to me. The words went like this: "Blessed Savior, keep me humble as I travel day-by-day." When I consider Genie's circumstances in light of his heartfelt request, I believe his life reflects the true meaning of humility. He later asked that I forgive him for "getting choked up" while recording one of the other songs, for the words so reminded him of his mother's love and childhood days.

After extensive hours of practice, Genie gained the needed confidence to accept a friend's invitation to play guitar in public. He looked forward to their practice sessions and their volunteer performances at nursing homes, where music became their witness.

Although I had never heard him sing in public, the highlight of several of my visits was Genie's private mini concert in his own yard. As soon as he removed his guitar from its case, I knew a blessing was on its way. The messages in his songs revealed his Christian faith. As he humbly played and sang, I felt God was listening too.

Because I love photography like Genie loves music, I longed to take additional pictures of him with his guitar. Although I was reluctant to ask, I am grateful that I did. Because of limited finances throughout his life, he recalled seldom having had his picture taken—once as a child and other times for photo IDs.

As soon as Genie removed his guitar from its case, I knew a blessing was on its way.

When Genie humbly played and sang, the messages in his songs revealed his Christian faith.

Genie felt very much at home as he strummed his guitar
and sang in the natural setting of his yard.

Weeks later, I made a return trip with my camera. As I pulled off to the side of the road next to his house, the first thing I noticed—thanks to his friend—was his newly mowed grass. In the distance I spotted Genie, seemingly ready and waiting, with guitar nearby.

To have a natural setting for his picture, Genie adjusted the firewood at the side of his house where the afternoon sun provided needed light. Although this was not the most comfortable place to sit, he felt very much at home as he strummed his guitar and sang in the natural setting of his yard. I shot pictures, many pictures, trying to capture the peace and contentment that music brought to his life.

Considering his substandard living conditions, society would not understand how Genie could possibly experience contentment, especially when viewing the front and back entrances to his house. Many of the boards on his front porch had deteriorated over time. The extra weight of unused firewood on the rotted boards had caused it to collapse, making his front entrance inaccessible.

I had never noticed the unsafe condition of his back entrance until rain complicated one of my earlier visits, forcing me to use his back steps. How well I remember that day—

There had been rain that day, lots and lots of rain. When my husband and I finally reached Genie's house, it looked abandoned. I wondered if he still lived here.

After we pulled off the highway into his yard, I sat in our car and thought, *Okay, God, what now?* As the steady rain continued to pound on the car, I focused on my destination—Genie's back door. Grass and weeds had grown knee-high and taller, leaving no visible path to that entrance.

Trying to escape the direct contact of the rain, I grabbed sacks of clothing and started raising my umbrella as I pushed open the

Realizing this was Genie's only usable entrance, I thought to myself, *Everybody deserves better than this!*

car door. With no detectable path, I hurriedly stepped through unmowed grass toward the back of his lot.

Rain had saturated the ground. With each step, I could feel water seeping into my sandals, which caused a squishy sound as I walked. Besides my feet becoming uncomfortably wet, tall weeds and gusts of wind made it impossible to keep the lower half of me dry. When I lifted the front of my umbrella just enough to see where I was headed, I spotted Genie waiting at his back entrance.

As soon as we were close enough to speak, Genie offered me shelter from the rain. After glancing at those steps, I thanked him but politely declined. I assured him I would be fine as long as I had my umbrella. Instead of climbing those stairs to his back door, I remained at ground level and handed up the sacks of clothing for him to try on. While I waited under my umbrella, my eyes focused on his back entrance in disbelief.

The sight of those steps was most disturbing. The warped boards looked so wobbly and rotten. I noticed a large stick propped against a weathered two-by-four, probably placed there with the intention of extra support. Realizing this was Genie's only usable entrance, I thought to myself, *Everybody deserves better than this!*

As I continued to wait, I glanced across his lot. I remembered how this yard had always been our common meeting ground. It was here that food and clothing had been transferred to him routinely. If the weather was extremely hot or cold, we just talked a little faster and cut our visit a little shorter, but never before had it rained like this on a visit. This was not the typical day—rain and more rain!

Over the tapping of the rain on his metal roof, I thought, *What? Was that singing?* I could make out the faint melody of his voice as he tried on the clothing inside his house. Although I couldn't recognize distinct words, I knew for certain there was a song in his heart.

After he switched sizes several times, Genie appeared at his back door wearing khaki pants and a western-style shirt with tags still attached. We agreed that the outfit was a definite fit, a good choice for his guitar-playing sessions at the nursing home.

With the rain beating harder, Genie insisted that I wait inside his back door. I hesitated at first because of the unsafe steps, but then I proceeded cautiously. Under the protection of his roof, I returned the unneeded clothing to the appropriate sacks. After we said our good-byes and wished each other well, I raised my umbrella and headed back to the car.

~~~

What Genie lacks in material possessions is nothing compared to the richness of his faith. He trusts God that everything will be okay. Because of his lack of materialism, society considers him a loser. But because of God's grace and the acceptance of Jesus in his heart, I believe him to be a winner. Genie's friendship is one of the most inspiring relationships in my life—a real blessing and a step up in faith.

CHAPTER THREE

Journey of Hope

The desperate cry of a homeless family resulted in tender moments and heart-changing experiences.

What an eye-opener! A homeless family with three small boys and a baby had spent the night in a cornfield, sleeping in the bed of their worn-out truck. They had no food, no source of water, and no shelter. With pocket money nearly gone, their future was bleak.

The following morning, the desperate father tried to find a way to survive. He spoke to the owner of a nearby farm supply store, which was conveniently located less than a mile up the road. The owner agreed to do what she could, and being a friend of mine, she counted on my help.

After talking with her on the phone, I thought, *Living in the bed of an old truck, not a camper but a truck! How can this be?* Their circumstances were absolutely destitute.

News of their plight spread quickly throughout the surrounding area. That same morning, neighboring families donated food. By midafternoon, a local farmer had offered the use of his vacant tenant house in exchange for labor. Even though their circumstances seemed to be improving, I decided to make the twenty-mile trip to see the situation firsthand.

This family was a pitiful sight, worse than I had imagined. A reddish rash covered their fair-skinned bodies, evidence of mite bites contracted while they had been working on a chicken farm in Texas. Their dirty, matted hair needed shampooing, and it was obvious that baths and showers had been lacking for days. The troubled expressions on their faces and the sadness in their eyes revealed a real cry for help.

After talking with the dad, I took a mental inventory of their limited possessions, which lay in ruin in the back of their truck. Without the covering of a tarp, their two dirty and worn-out mattresses had been rained on and baked by the sun during their trip all the way from Texas to Kentucky. Although they owned no beds, the father explained that he and his wife slept on the double mattress, his three small sons shared the one twin mattress, and the baby slept on nothing but a folded-up blanket. They owned no furniture, no appliances, no TV—nothing of value.

To make matters worse, when I tried to separate their dirty clothing from past weeks for laundering, I found many items not salvageable. The soiled clothing that had been left in torn trash bags in the back of their truck and exposed intermittently to sun and rain was beginning to rot. They owned no other clothing except that on their backs. I checked their sizes, assuring them of help the following day.

Early the next morning, lack of running water made baths impossible, but clean-smelling clothes replaced the worn. Bags of soiled clothing filled my trunk. With baby in arms, the mother rounded up the small children for a trip with me to the local Laundromat.

As I stood beside the washing machines, I learned the truth. The father, not the mother, did the family laundry. I soon understood why. She could neither read the directions for using the machines nor count out coins. Although she lacked the skills to do this task, she tried her best to learn.

It soon became obvious that indoor plumbing was a luxury for this family. Because they had never lived in housing with a bathroom, the small children constantly used the corner of any room for this purpose. Trying to change the routine behavior of three little boys certainly tested my patience! Cleaning the commode was another learning experience for the mother. As she reached down into the toilet bowl with her bare hand, I quickly stopped her. She didn't know that a brush and cleaner were available to help her do the job.

~~~

Alerting people from a small community church about this family's lack of necessities resulted in much generosity. Several truckloads of needed items were soon delivered and immediately unloaded: baby crib, beds and mattresses, refrigerator, stove, table and chairs, sofa, food, clothing, towels, toys. The list went on.

When bedtime rolled around that evening, a special place awaited each family member. After a warm bath, the baby spent her first night sleeping in a crib while snuggling with a newly adopted toy. Then, one by one, the little guys received a bath and shampoo and put on clean pajamas before being tucked in, each on his very own mattress. Because of a donated bed, the parents also had a more comfortable place to sleep. Everyone counted their blessings—those who gave and those who received. We left for home that night with thankful hearts, knowing we, too, would have a more peaceful night's rest.

~~~

Because the tenant house had not been occupied during the past several years, knee-high grass and weeds had taken control of the yard. Mowing even a small section wasn't an easy job, but it allowed the children a decent place to play. Laughter could be heard as healing brought relief to their irritated skin.

This family didn't go unnoticed. Concerned people kept in contact with them, helping with their needs. They were blessed with food and gifts, especially during the fall and winter holidays.

Then one day in early spring, the tenant house was found empty. No one ever saw them again.

~~~

I can't give an answer for why this family pulled up stakes and hit the road again in a worn-out truck after seemingly living a better life. But that's not for me to figure out. Perhaps it was just as God had intended, for He sometimes places people in our lives for only a season to help care for them and to give them hope.

One particular regret lingers in my heart. The mother had told me she wanted to learn how to read the words in their new picture Bible. Although this was never accomplished during those months, hopefully, with the help of the pictures, she could recall the stories read to her and her children about Jesus and eternal life.

God used His people to help care for this fragile family and to deliver His hope to them—hope found in Jesus. Life is just that, a journey of hope.

CHAPTER FOUR

Challenges and Trouble

From the act of stealing to the click of a handcuff, I saw it all as I became involved in children's ministry.

Challenging did not adequately describe the job of children's coordinator at a small community church. A big gap existed between what was being done and what needed to be done. My heart told me to include children living in low-income housing, even though a few members thought otherwise. Children, not comfort zones, became the focus of our ministry.

In order for children from the projects to attend Sunday school, they would need transportation. The church agreed to let us use their van, which ordinarily sat idle in the parking lot from week to week. But a van without a qualified driver would get us nowhere. Thankfully, the local jailer volunteered to fill this position. The drawbacks seemed few, and a vision soon turned into action when a dedicated youth named Johnny accompanied me to the projects.

It was pleasantly warm that Saturday morning, the kind of day that naturally draws neighboring people—especially children—to the outdoors. The brightness of the sun cast shadows that kept in step with us, and the vivid blue sky added to the joy of the day. Our unfamiliar presence attracted attention, but we didn't remain strangers for long. The hours we spent walking, talking, and inviting the children to Sunday school, as well as seeking support and permission from parents and guardians, resulted in a van filled with young passengers the following morning.

One of these families had four children, ages ten and under, with another on the way. For weeks, these youngsters faithfully attended Sunday school. The morning they didn't arrive on the van, I became concerned and called their home, thinking they might still need a ride.

The dad answered the phone. In a rather gruff-sounding voice, he blamed the children for oversleeping. I could hear their emotional pleas and cries of disappointment in the background, but the dad denied them a second chance.

These children seemed starved for attention and often lacked confidence in themselves. At times, I would drop by their place on Saturdays to help them read out of their picture Bibles. In this way, their mother, Barbara, could hear about Jesus too. The children would huddle around a small coffee table inside their front door, nearly sitting on top of one another, books open, ready to learn.

Even though Barbara couldn't read, she eagerly participated as if competing with her children. During our discussions about the Bible stories, she would often blurt out answers, many of which were wrong. To help her learn more about Jesus, I invited her to help me at Sunday school during the upcoming weeks. That brought about bigger challenges—

One morning, Barbara didn't leave the building after Sunday school was dismissed. Instead, while others attended church, this expectant mother not only helped herself to some baby clothes specifically donated for a mission project in the mountains but also stole part of the Sunday offering for that day.

As soon as church was over, news of her dishonesty circulated quickly. Within minutes, members of the church administration confronted her at her house and demanded that she return the stolen items. When she flatly denied their accusations, they left empty-handed. Hearing about this incident left me disappointed and discouraged. Because I had invited her, I felt responsible and made a similar trip.

Unsure if she would even talk to me, I knocked on her door. She answered and politely invited me in. Although I couldn't predict her next move, I knew by her action that a certain bond of friendship still existed. I wanted her to feel my support but correct her own wrongdoing.

In a direct but caring way, I explained that returning items that didn't belong to her wasn't a matter of choice but just the right thing to do. I let her know that I, too, might be blamed if the items didn't reappear. Without saying a word, she turned and quietly left the room. I stood there anxiously waiting in hopes of a change of heart.

As she reentered the room, I caught a glimpse of something in her hands. Without hesitation, she handed over the missing baby clothes and the money. To my surprise, along with these stolen items came an apology. Her words and action made her appear trustworthy, but somehow, I sensed the *real* Barbara hadn't changed. Even so, I was thankful her heart had convinced her to be truthful, if only for the moment. Because of this incident, Barbara chose to remain at home on Sunday mornings but allowed the children to come to Sunday school.

~~~

A few weeks later, dishonesty hit again! While I was shopping in a local grocery, out of the corner of my eye, I spotted two of Barbara's children hurriedly zigzagging down an aisle, dodging customers and shopping carts before purposely running out of the store with women's purses, which obviously did not belong to them! Sadly enough, Barbara had taught her eight- and ten-year-old children to steal purses out of unattended grocery carts while she waited for them in the getaway car.

Knowing I could identify those children, I hung around for a while after the rather irate store manager phoned the police. He tried to be friendly as we engaged in conversation, but the look of disgust remained on his face. He seemed somewhat embarrassed having to admit, "This isn't the first time these kids and their mom pulled this stunt and got away with it!"

I thought to myself, *The same store, the same plan, the same participants—surely not!* Knowing that the police knew the names of this family, I didn't understand how they had managed to escape the law.

I felt miserable knowing Barbara had involved her kids in breaking the law, but neither she nor her children had seen me shopping in the grocery that day. There were no witnesses to report this to our church, and I said nothing. I felt an even greater need to continue the job I had started. I assumed responsibility for her children being at Sunday school, and our lives went on as if this had never happened.

~~~

I had become a stay-at-home mom after the birth of our baby. For six or seven months, I had avoided the thirty-mile drive to a neighboring town to shop. For some unknown reason, I awoke one Saturday morning and thought it would be fun for the three of us to make that trip.

I told my husband about wanting to go to a particular baby store that I had never been to, even though I didn't plan on buying anything. By the look of confusion on his face, I realized the idea of shopping with no intention of buying seemed absolutely senseless to him. Although certainly not to his way of thinking, he agreed to take me anyway.

As we arrived in that town, I insisted on stopping there first. After we located the store, I anxiously opened the door and walked in, still feeling the strong tug at my heart to be there. I expected to see many moms and their children busily shopping, but that was not so.

I seemed to be the only customer, but then I noticed two policemen who had detained some people in the back of the store. I felt out of place and thought of leaving, but after I observed that scene more closely, I could hardly believe my eyes—there stood Barbara with two of her children!

Absolute quiet blanketed the entire sales floor except for their voices. One officer recorded answers on a clipboard as he and a fellow officer questioned Barbara. When she answered to a name other than her own, a red flag went up. I knew she had given a fake identity.

I could no longer be silent, but neither did I want to totally destroy her trust. Unsure of how to handle this situation, I walked to the back of the store and intentionally asked, "Barbara, is there anything I can do to help?"

Because she had been standing with her back toward the entrance, she was unaware of my presence. My question caught her off-guard. When she responded to her real name, the police picked up on her fake identity. Knowing she had been caught in the act, she confessed to giving false information.

Within minutes, one of the policemen instructed Barbara to put her hands behind her back and handcuffed her before he escorted her out of the store as a criminal. I could hardly watch as her two young daughters—both members of my Sunday school class—walked quietly beside their mother without a hand to hold. Even though only first- and third-graders and seemingly innocent, both were probably guilty of assisting their mom.

While one officer accompanied them to the police car, the other remained inside. He requested additional information. My heart reminded me to tell the truth even when it hurt—the same lesson I had tried to teach Barbara. I explained our past connections and her history of dishonesty, especially when it involved her children. After he finished his report, the officer thanked me and headed out the door toward his vehicle.

I didn't feel comfortable walking out of the store until the police car started to pull out of the parking lot. By that time, I felt somewhat abandoned and emotionally drained. I knew the click of those handcuffs would cause us to travel different paths. But through it all, I was intensely aware of God's presence. As we, too, left the parking lot, I couldn't help but wonder what would become of their lives in the days ahead.

Several hours later, when our car was waiting at a stop sign in another section of town, a squad car turned the corner directly in front of us. It was headed for the drive-through window at a fast food restaurant. There in the backseat sat Barbara with two of her daughters, about to have their last meal together before their separation. Barbara's freedom was over, at least temporarily. As we drove off in opposite directions, mixed emotions and endless remembrances filled my heart. I never saw Barbara or any of her children again.

The next day was Sunday, but it didn't seem like a Sunday. I left for Sunday school feeling sad and concerned. I knew Barbara's kids were home without a mom and supervised by a dad who regarded Sunday school as unimportant. To make matters worse, I dreaded hearing remarks regarding the previous day's arrest.

I had no more than stepped inside the church when a board member met me with the question, "Do you know Barbara was caught shoplifting yesterday and arrested?"

To her surprise and mine, I humbly answered, "Yes, I watched it." Our conversation ended, and Barbara was never mentioned again.

~~~

Barbara served a two-year sentence in a women's correctional facility. Soon after her release, I received a totally unexpected call. Barbara phoned to tell me about her improved family situation. They had left the projects and had moved to a trailer in the country. After she said, "We're changing our lives for the better," she thanked me for being her friend. I wasn't exactly sure what her comments implied, but considering all that God had allowed us to go through together, being called her friend left an impact on my heart.

I had walked alongside Barbara and her children for a short season of life, not by chance but by faith after hearing God's call. His perfectly timed direction allowed me to witness the stealing of purses at a local grocery and the handcuffing of Barbara in a town some thirty miles up the road. These godly encounters still weigh heavily on my heart and challenge my faith to accept truth beyond human understanding. How God directs the Holy Spirit to connect us during such events is unexplainable, a mystery—not ours to fully understand.

Barbara spent time behind bars and experienced limited freedom and isolation from society but not separation from the unconditional love of God. Perhaps prison was the wake-up call Barbara needed to turn her life around. Maybe she sensed God in our friendship. Maybe—just maybe—that quiet time helped convince her heart of the love of Jesus and the need for God's forgiveness. That is my hope and prayer, but only God knows.

CHAPTER FIVE

Each One Counts

A trip across town for just one child? I thank God the response had been yes.

The van ministry at a small community church involved children from low-income housing. One location was nearby; the other, across town. To begin this outreach, a devoted high school student named Johnny joined me one Saturday morning to walk the streets of those neighborhoods—particularly the one closest to our church—to personally invite children of all ages to come to Sunday school.

The following morning, the church van slowly traveled up and down those same streets, making repeated stops for young riders to climb aboard. It became nearly filled with passengers before heading across town to pick up one last child.

Even though there was little Sunday morning traffic, it seemed like forever getting to our destination. I began to question whether or not we could justify driving the extra miles for just one child. But I didn't question for long, because I already knew the answer.

After the van turned into the housing project, I began looking for a steep lot. I soon caught sight of our last little passenger, a first-grader waiting beside his mother outside their front door. When the van began to slow, she released him to catch his ride.

His strong little legs came hurrying down several flights of concrete steps at full speed to the sidewalk below. After he climbed up into the van, he intentionally found a seat next to a window so he could watch his mother wave until she was out of sight. Although he spoke few words to anyone, he shared his contagious grin.

~~~

One Sunday morning, this same little guy slipped quietly into the classroom a few minutes early like some of his friends. He sat down at his usual place at the table and waited for the rest of his classmates to arrive. As I turned to greet him, I noticed something unusual about the top of his left cheek. It looked puffed out, much larger than the other. I joked with him a little, thinking he might be hiding a big wad of chewing gum there.

At the mention of the word *gum*, he smiled back while he shook his head no. Instead of speaking, he widely opened his mouth and wiggled his tongue around in all directions to prove his truthfulness. When I realized that no gum existed, the joking abruptly ended. Our conversation took on a more serious tone.

He was a child of few words but not that day. Starting with an incident at school, he told me everything he could remember happening. He had accidentally bumped his face on another student's desk. The appearance of an unusual lump concerned his mother enough to consult a doctor. After examination, the attending physician advised them to keep an eye on the area, thinking it might disappear on its own. All they could do was wait.

~~~

Weeks passed, but the lump remained. There was no sign of

noticeable improvement. Because of the doctor's growing concern, he referred him to a specialist at a large metropolitan hospital. At that scheduled visit, doctors took biopsies, ordered lab work, and then confirmed the sad diagnosis. His battle to fight cancer began.

Doctors performed immediate surgery. As soon as he awoke from his operation, the mother asked someone to phone me. Hearing his diagnosis brought much heartache and concern, especially for one so young. I didn't expect the long-distance call or her referring to me as best friend. In fact, I had seldom spoken with the mother. Perhaps making that trip across town and including her young son meant more to her than I had realized.

Sunday school wasn't the same without him. His absence left sadness in our hearts. His empty chair reminded us of the pain and treatments he had to endure. Each week we prayed that God would help heal our little friend.

~~~

Months later, when his treatments were nearing an end, I thought I had several weeks to prepare the children for his return. My assumption was wrong—

One Sunday, he came rushing into the classroom unexpectedly, so excited to be back. He wore no cap to hide his loss of hair, but his God-given smile helped to camouflage his pain. Although his presence caught all of us by surprise, his classmates gathered around him and greeted him warmly as if nothing were different.

At the end of our lesson that day, one of his classmates named Jonathan scooted up out of his chair, leaned over the table on one elbow, and anxiously waved his hand in the air. He asked to say a prayer all by himself for the friend sitting beside him. When he did, the room went silent. Hands were folded. Eyes were closed. God heard a beautiful prayer from a loving and compassionate heart.

Now that our friend had returned, when the bell rang and told us it was time to go, we wished Sunday school could have lasted a little longer. The best lesson taught was by the children themselves—their love and acceptance and prayers for a friend who was fighting for his life.

Within months, my family and I moved some distance away. We hadn't lived there long before I received a phone call from a dear friend of our former church. When I heard the words "bad news," I knew the reason for her call. This brave child's battle with cancer had ended. Many hearts grieved. I could only imagine the pain and deep sorrow that this single mother endured over the loss of her only child.

~~~

I thank God for His gentle promptings to reach one more for Jesus. Although saddened by the death of our little friend, I am thankful for the friends he had found in Sunday school and even more thankful for the friend he had found in Jesus.

Although he had lived for only a short time here on earth, his heart belonged to Jesus, the most important relationship in anyone's lifetime. Because of his faith, God assured him of a continued life in heaven, healed of all pain and disease.

That same gift of eternal life is offered to everyone here on earth. We must continue sharing the message of the cross, for each one counts.

CHAPTER SIX

"Don't Touch My Card!"

Finding ways to brighten the lives of nursing home residents during the Christmas season can be a challenge, but when music fills the air, who knows what will happen?

Christmas was fast approaching. Time was running out for all the shopping, the baking, and especially the card-writing. But despite the busyness of the season, the residents at a local nursing home needed to feel loved and remembered too.

Walking the hallways equipped with handrails to aid the elderly was quite a contrast from walking the crowded malls amid holiday shoppers. Instead of seeing commercialism and hurriedness, I noticed the slow-paced lives and the obvious challenges of those around me. For some, separation from loved ones and a home of their own made the upcoming holiday seem not the least bit like Christmas. Many found the joy of the season intermingled with pain, loneliness, and a sense of hopelessness.

To help brighten their holiday, the ladies at my church made colorful lap covers so all residents would receive at least one special gift, whether they realized it was Christmas or not. Wrapping them in decorative paper and adding shiny bows gave each a special touch. But in spite of the gifts, something was missing—something to remind them of the true meaning of Christmas.

Days later, the thought occurred to me: *Christmas cards! Why not give each a musical Christmas card?* I knew the problem wouldn't be the lack of cards in the stores but the lack of meaning in the cards. No snowmen, Santa, or flying reindeer would do. Instead, pictured on the front must be baby Jesus, and when opened, a meaningful carol must play.

Buying musical cards seemed like a good idea at the time, but imagining the sound of forty such cards being opened simultaneously in a rather small and crowded lobby was a bit unsettling. I feared the intended sounds of carols might result in indescribable noise. Although the administration gave their approval, they did so with a smile.

With the support of parents, young children from my Sunday school class helped with this project. When they opened the musical cards to print "God Loves You" in big letters, the sounds of repetitive carols and children's giggles filled the classroom. Everyone looked forward to this upcoming event.

~~~

On the day of our planned visit, the frigid temperature was typical of the wintry season ahead. After parents unloaded young passengers in front of the facility, bare hands grasped the cold metal railing as little feet anxiously climbed the steps leading to the lobby.

Once inside, the children could hardly wait to give each resident a specially wrapped package. But for some children, it didn't stop there. They proceeded to help unwrap the gift, unfold the cover, and carefully drape it over the resident's lap, which caused strangers to become friends.

The children's helpfulness continued as they passed out the

cards. Thinking only they knew the secret of how to activate the music, they repeatedly opened and closed the cards until the residents began doing this for themselves.

Amid the commotion, a mixture of laughter and music filled the lobby. Faces brightened and hearts responded with joy. Some of the residents began singing and humming the familiar tunes, spreading Christmas cheer in their own special way. Others proudly shared the words inside their cards with those around them, not realizing everyone's card had the exact same message. By this time, I wasn't sure who wore the biggest smiles, the children giving the cards or the elderly receiving them . . . or perhaps the staff!

Before we left, we visited those residents confined to rooms and gave them each a lap cover and a card. As we exited through the lobby and said our good-byes, the children took with them a new awareness of the less remembered and the lonely.

~~~

The following week, I received a note on a Christmas card that read, "Words can never express how I appreciate your sending the musical Christmas cards. My husband has been a patient there for a year. He is an Alzheimer's victim and responds very little. When given the card, he held it close to him and would not turn it loose. It mattered not what they did to him as long as they didn't bother his card."

Days after reading her note, my heart kept recalling her message. I felt the need to phone her. As she began to speak, she painfully shared how her husband's behavior had become progressively mean and hateful over the years, which is common with this disease. His refusal to cooperate with family and staff made it extremely difficult for caregivers and family members to show their love. She expressed amazement at how his meanness had turned to gentleness after he had received the musical card.

Before our conversation ended, she told me about her new hope. After she had seen firsthand what research had proven—that music seemed to have a soothing effect on patients with Alzheimer's—she planned on adding music to part of her husband's daily therapy.

When I think about all of the extensive research and expensive medications prescribed to ease the minds of Alzheimer's victims, I remember that patient, the musical card, and his only request, "Don't touch my card!"

CHAPTER SEVEN

In Need of the Savior

Many experiences in life are considered coincidences. But perhaps God connects our lives with those of strangers more often than we realize—sometimes for a short season and at other times for a lifetime.

Minnie and her young son, like many living in a nearby rural community, struggled at times to make ends meet. Even buying affordable clothing became somewhat of a hardship. Through this need, our lives became connected.

Conveniently located in that same rural area was a newly opened farm supply store that was owned and operated by a young friend of mine. She had a big heart when it came to helping others, especially children. She was well aware of the needs of local people and sometimes shared those concerns with me.

Several times throughout the year, she agreed to let me use part of the large storage area in the back of her store as a distribution center for free used clothing. It provided both a clean and accessible location. But this outreach wouldn't have been possible without the generous donations of a small community church some twenty miles away.

During those particular days, the back room took on a more store-like appearance. Instead of rushing in and rummaging through the clothing, neighboring families arrived at their scheduled times and politely waited their turns to be helped. Minnie, her son, and her two brothers benefited from the generosity of others, as did many local families. At times, matching the donated clothing to people's specific needs seemed more than coincidental.

The findings for one family, in particular, seemed rather incredible. The petite mother, who wore a size four, seriously doubted she'd find clothing to fit her. But my helper in Sunday school had donated a large box of exceptionally beautiful clothing of that exact size. After I outfitted the young mother and both of her little girls, I spoke with the husband. He needed most a pair of size-eleven dress shoes so he could attend church with his family. Only one pair had been donated. That pair of new-looking dress shoes—which happened to be his size—fit him perfectly.

A women's coat proved to be another unusual match. An elderly lady with a crippled hand needed a medium-sized, lightweight coat, one suitable to wear to church on cool mornings. When we checked the women's rack, we found only one. The cream-colored coat looked practically new and met her specifications—lightweight and size medium. I removed the coat from the hanger for her to try on. Using the strength from her good hand, she raised her crippled hand high enough to slip it into the sleeve of the coat. She stood there smiling, thankful that it fit. Time and time again, the donated clothing took on new ownership in an amazing way.

~~~

At Christmas time, special gifts were bought for Minnie's family and those who had participated in the clothing giveaways. After I made the last home delivery, my trunk became empty, but one sack remained in the backseat of my car. It contained two cuddly baby dolls. I had purchased them earlier that day, having no one in mind. I now questioned my motive for buying them.

I glanced again at the backseat and thought, *Surely, there must be someone who could use the dolls.* But Minnie, having only one son, certainly had no need for them. All the little girls on our list had been given presents. I could think of no other contacts. Even though it was after business hours and becoming dark, I decided to stop by the farm supply store in hopes that my friend might still be at work and could suggest a home for them.

When I pulled up in front of the store, I noticed a faint glimmer of light in the back part of the building. But before I could open my car door, an old and worn-out car pulled up next to me. It was too dark to make out the details of the people inside, but the security light allowed me to see the silhouette of a mother holding a baby on the passenger's side.

As the driver stepped out of his vehicle and headed toward the store, the same overhead light drew attention to his worn, shabby clothing. I, too, got out of my car and asked if I could be of help. He said that he needed to use a phone. As he continued walking toward the front entrance, I returned to my vehicle, not knowing quite what to do. Even though the store was closed for the day, my friend allowed him to go inside to make his call.

While I waited in my car, I was surprised to see a pair of little eyes peeking out from the back window of the vehicle parked next to me. When I remembered the sack in the backseat of my car, I began to wonder—

Regardless of the cold night air, I approached the mother. She politely rolled down her window far enough for us to speak. One glance inside the car convinced me of their financial hardship. Our conversation was brief. She told me she had two daughters— the young child sitting in the backseat and the baby resting in her arms. After I told her about the contents of my sack, she replied, "I'm sure both would love to have a baby doll for Christmas."

Before they drove off, I handed the sack though the open window to the smiling mother, amazed at how the two baby dolls had found a home for Christmas.

~~~

The following year, the list of recipients increased. Because of the growing number of people, we asked Minnie and the other families to pick up their gifts in the back room of the store. A message sharing the true meaning of Christmas was part of every gift.

On the day of the distribution, by the time everything was wrapped and loaded, I was running about a half an hour late. I phoned the store to assure those waiting families that I would be there shortly.

Being overly tired, I dreaded the twenty-mile trip. I imagined kids running wild in the back of the store and their parents irritated and pacing the floor, wishing I would hurry up and get there. I visualized paper being ripped off specially wrapped packages in a matter of seconds and perhaps people not even liking their gifts. Actually, I wished this to be over!

When I pulled into the parking lot, extra vehicles assured me I was not too late. But as I opened the back door to walk in, I heard no voices. Once inside, I found everyone, including the children, seated on stored boxes of merchandise or feed sacks, quietly waiting. I apologized for being late, but no one seemed to mind.

As family names were called to receive their box of gifts, my focus turned to Minnie. She and her young son sat close beside one another on one of the unopened boxes of merchandise. Her dark bangs hung down slightly over the top of her eyes. She never looked up, or at least I couldn't tell if she did. I didn't know why, but this lady touched my heart in a very special way.

My attention turned to a desperate mother of four. Standing beside me with tear-filled eyes, she explained her family's unfortunate situation. Her husband was serving time in jail for driving to work on an expired license. He had lacked the money to renew it—and still couldn't afford it. The authorities had agreed to release him to go to work during the day if he returned each night and shared his pay. She had already admitted to the children that there was little money and that they would have to celebrate Christmas without presents. As she was handed their box of gifts, the children rushed to her side. The mother's kind words and the expressions on their faces revealed their thankful hearts.

One by one, families claimed their presents. When Minnie and the other recipients left, each carried their box of unopened gifts to their vehicle with the intention of saving them for Christmas. The back room of the store became quiet once again, filled with memories of loving hugs, kind words, and tender moments.

~~~

Months later, a change in my husband's job meant moving to a new location over a hundred miles away. When my church family who had donated the clothing asked how I could leave Minnie and the other special people from that community, I didn't have an answer. I wanted to tell them good-bye in person, so one Saturday before our move, my husband drove me to that area.

As we approached the home of a young newlywed couple, I

spotted their truck kicking up dust as it traveled our direction down their long gravel driveway. When they reached our vehicle, they stopped to talk. The wife sat snuggled close beside her husband on the driver's side, and on the passenger's seat laid a black Bible. They excitedly shared their testimonies about recently being saved at a revival at a small country church.

We continued on our way, making stops at various homes throughout the community. Family after family reported the same wonderful news. They named family members and friends who had accepted Christ, including the man who owned the new dress shoes and the dad who had spent his nights in jail, along with his entire family!

Minnie told me about accepting Christ when her son was about eight years old. "One night at a revival in a small country church, my neighbor and good friend came back to talk to me. As I made my first step from behind the bench to go to the altar, I believe that was when the Lord saved me. I don't remember getting to the altar. Making that first step for the Lord is all it takes. There were eight of us at the time, including my older brother."

Seeing and hearing about their changed lives lifted my spirits. Many of these people needed more than clothes and material items; they were in need of the Savior. I thanked God that those who weren't already Christian were saved. I knew now how I could leave. I could leave with peace in my heart, knowing that those who were in need of the Savior had found Him.

~~~

After I had moved some distance away, I lost contact with most of these people with the exception of Minnie. For the past twenty-five years, phone calls, uplifting cards, and special visits keep us in touch. We share our ups and our downs, our happy times and our sad. She always listens and responds with a caring and encouraging heart.

Minnie not only remains my dear spiritual friend and prayer partner but also lovingly fulfills her special roles as wife, mother, and grandmother. Although she no longer serves as a teacher on Sunday mornings, she faithfully attends Sunday school and church. As she wrote in one of her letters, "I love reading and studying about my Savior."

In a recent phone call during the Christmas season, we reminisced a little about our past. Minnie commented that the two jackets given to her brothers one Christmas nearly twenty-five years ago had gone through much wear and numerous washings. One jacket had finally worn out this past season. But the other one—saved to be worn mostly on Sundays—received a final washing before they passed it on in hopes of keeping another warm.

She then spoke of the angel placed at the top of her Christmas tree, reminding me of a gift I had given her many years ago. I tried to visualize it from her description. The angel had curly hair, wore a gold-colored dress, held an opened songbook, and looked as though she were singing. As we finished our talk on the phone, I thanked God for His real angels and for my lifelong friend.

The giving of jackets and angels and gifts is a special part of Christmas. But Minnie will agree—nothing is as important as sharing our faith and telling others about Jesus. Everyone is in need of the Savior.

CHAPTER EIGHT

My Last Christmas

Earthly gifts no longer interested my elderly friend. With Jesus in her heart, she waited on God's heavenly promise.

Nursing homes are lonely, even at Christmas. Family members and friends may find less time to visit because of holiday plans. Sometimes a job or distance or bad weather might make a visit unlikely. There always seem to be a few residents who have no family ties or close acquaintances. Regardless of the number of visitors, a certain amount of sadness exists among the residents because of failing health and lack of mobility.

Sometimes I hesitate to make my visits, too. However, when I stop by a local nursing home on a regular basis, faces become familiar. The more frequent the visits, the closer the relationships and the greater my attachment to the residents.

I checked on one elderly lady who had become a grandmother figure to me. She shared many special thoughts close to her heart, and sadness overwhelmed me the day she told me about the radical surgery needed on her legs.

For her, this dreaded procedure was a life-saving choice. But through it all, she knew there would be no getting better, just surviving a little longer. My heart ached, aware of her extreme pain and discomfort. But regardless of her suffering, her faith made life bearable and gave her a sense of peace and hope.

With Christmas drawing near, I wanted my dear friend and

the other residents to be remembered in a special way. I counted on the young children in my Sunday school class to help make this happen.

Excitement filled our classroom as we busily prepared for our visit. The children printed "Jesus loves you" along with their names inside each card. We practiced singing the first verse of Christmas carols over and over again, trying to memorize the words and also the tunes. Regardless of our efforts, not all voices blended, and not all words were remembered; however, that didn't stop us from carrying out our plans.

Before our visit, I prepared the children in other ways. I explained about poor health and people being sick and maybe not even friendly. I told them about some people who would have their legs in casts and about my elderly friend, who had very short legs because of an operation. The look of understanding on their faces told me they would adjust better to these situations than many adults, including me.

~~~

The day of our planned visit, parents supervised as anxious children quickly climbed out of heated cars into the chilled air and huddled together on their way to the lobby. Although it was decorated with a Christmas theme, the Christmas spirit seemed missing. Distressed looks covered the faces of many.

Most of the elderly sat side-by-side in chairs that lined the outside walls. Others confined to wheelchairs crowded together in the center of this small lobby, leaving barely enough room for the children to squeeze between them. Regardless of where residents sat, most were quietly waiting, while a few had nodded off to sleep.

As residents caught a glimpse of the young visitors, a gradual transformation took place. The big smiles on their little faces were contagious as they placed Christmas cards in the waiting hands and laps of residents. Soon, the children's voices filled the lobby with familiar carols, sharing the true meaning of Christmas.

When the interaction came to an end, smiles were exchanged and thank you's were said. A feeling of love bridged the gap between the young and the elderly, which allowed the Christmas spirit to come alive. But even greater challenges lay ahead. Our hearts would be further tested while ministering love and hope to the bedridden patients.

A nurse led the way, peeking into rooms and nodding as our sign of approval to enter. The children continued sharing cards and singing favorite requests. We followed the same procedure, and all went well until the nurse hurriedly walked past a slightly darkened room without even stopping. The familiarity of this room left me nearly in tears.

I consulted the nurse, who explained that the elderly lady in critical condition no longer responded to anyone. I told her of our close friendship and convinced her of our need to sing, even if she couldn't hear us.

As we entered her room, there was no doubt. The bedcovers revealed that this was my special friend. Even though her eyes stayed closed, the children quietly surrounded her bedside and sang their very best as if she could hear every word. I felt certain that she could, even though she showed no visible signs.

After the children ended their singing with "Silent Night," they politely placed Christmas cards on her quilt, thinking she could read them when she awoke from her nap. I nodded to them in approval, and they quietly moved to the hallway.

Because I was the last to leave and realized her grave condition, I tried to hide my tears as I glanced back at my friend. At that moment, I noticed her lips moving as if she were trying to speak.

When I drew close, her weary eyes slightly blinked. In a barely audible voice, she thanked me for bringing the children to sing. Her final words to me were spoken in a hushed whisper: "This is my last Christmas, you know."

As my elderly friend celebrated her last Christmas, she not only pictured Jesus as a baby lying in a manger but also anticipated seeing Him face-to-face as her Savior in heaven. Amid her discomfort and pain, indescribable peace and joy were hers.

CHAPTER NINE

"Just Not Today"

Each day is a gift but sometimes a hard one to accept because of life's unpredictable circumstances. But hidden in some of those most difficult days, one may find unexpected blessings.

Multiple sclerosis can be a devastating disease. Three of my former high school classmates were battling MS, and one's condition was becoming progressively worse. My heart struggled with the thought of paying her a visit.

When I heard that Nancy was being transferred to a nursing home for her final days, reality hit. I knew that could have been me. I had been given that diagnosis once. Days later, I became aware that a mistake had been made in the reading of my MRI. That life-changing experience left me emotionally drained but more sensitive to the needs of others, such as Nancy.

I remember that Nancy was so popular and attractive and admired by many during her former high school years. Now MS was slowly robbing her body of all muscular activity. The voice and limbs she had used as a cheerleader were becoming nonfunctional. *Why, God? Why such a drastic change in this person's life?*

For some unknown reason, I felt the need to connect with her. Yet, at the same time, I kept asking myself, *Why now, after all these years?*

Nearly twenty years ago back in my junior year, I transferred to the same high school Nancy attended, but our paths at school simply did not cross. Because we had never taken the same class or spoken a single word to each other, we had no connections. I rationalized that a visit would be awkward and uncomfortable; she simply would not know me.

Each trip back to my hometown, I used this reasoning time and time again to justify avoiding a visit. But then I would think, *Maybe I would go . . . just not today.* Weeks turned into months, but I made no attempt to visit.

~~~

One morning while I was staying with my mother, I awoke, knowing the day had come. No more excuses. No more delays. I felt I had to go see Nancy that very afternoon. It was as if the choice was no longer mine.

Not knowing her present condition, I prepared myself for the worst. Taking my baby was part of the plan. My mother agreed to care for him in the car until I found a directory and located her room.

As I stepped into the lobby, I felt much alone except for the two residents whose wheelchairs faced the entrance. It seemed rather quiet and empty for a facility of such size. I stood there, hesitating for a moment, thinking I heard something that sounded like my name. I heard it again.

I glanced to my right. The frail body sitting in the wheelchair was struggling to call out my name. As our eyes met, I slowly questioned, "Nancy?"

No directory was needed—she knew my name! From the position of her wheelchair, it seemed as though she had been expecting me. I didn't tell her I was coming. How did she know? I thought for a minute and remembered the perfect timing. I had my answer.

After I returned from the car with my baby, I joined Nancy in her room. Although I could barely understand her slurred speech, we seemed to communicate as much through our hearts as our words. I silently cheered her on as she deliberately tried to speak and move her limbs as normally as possible, although she got little results from her effort.

Aware of her fatigue, a skilled nurse carefully transferred her from her wheelchair to her bed. As this happened, I realized the tremendous effort and courage it took for her to cope each minute. My heart ached at the thought of this condition worsening, and I tried to block it from my mind.

By spending time with her that hour, God allowed me to better understand her condition. Her mind seemed alert and sharp but trapped inside a progressively weakening body. There was no way she could cope this well emotionally without the presence of God. Only He could account for such inner peace as she fought this battle for life on earth.

Before I left her room that day, we had a prayer and a hug. Holding my baby throughout this visit seemed to give me—actually both of us—a sense of comfort and joy, a blessing from God.

Through my sharing a day in her life, I was shown a new sense of peace available for the terminally ill. She experienced helplessness but not hopelessness. Life can rob us of physical abilities that we so often take for granted, but it cannot separate us from the unconditional love of God and His promise of eternal life, free of sickness and pain. Her healing would come later. I tucked this message inside my heart as I quietly left her room. I walked down the long hallway, holding my baby a little closer.

I was thankful for the gentle whisper to my heart that convinced me to visit her that day. Her humble life drew me closer to God. What a blessing I would have missed if I had again responded, "Just not today."

CHAPTER TEN

McDonald's Can Wait

*Several encounters with "Lady by the Lake" helped
shape a friendship and helped me see God's grace.*

My son, John, awoke happy and excited from his early
afternoon nap. I soon buckled him safely in his car seat, ready
to go to McDonald's for the ice cream and playtime he had been
promised. But as I reached to open my car door, my heart received
a simple but unexplainable message: Don't go!

This strong negative feeling overpowered my impulse to open
the door, and I pulled back my hand in disbelief. Even though it
made no sense to me, and certainly not to a three-year-old who
loved McDonald's, I postponed our trip.

Unbuckling his car seat before going anywhere certainly didn't
coincide with our original plans. As he slowly climbed out of his
seat to the concrete floor below, a few tears of disappointment
trickled down his cheeks. I knew a dish of vanilla ice cream would
be no substitute for a swirled cone, but that was my only available
offer. A gentle hug helped assure him that I wouldn't forget my
promise, even though for now, our trip to McDonald's would have
to wait.

After the two of us climbed the steps leading back into the
kitchen, I headed straight for the refrigerator a few feet away. But
before I had time to remove the carton of ice cream, the phone
rang. I quickly answered. The first words to reach my ear were, "I

was praying you'd be at home!"

The caller gave no name, but I recognized the voice. It belonged to an elderly lady, a dear church friend who lived in a cottage-style home beside a small lake. I knew her as Mrs. Gillette, but my son had renamed her "Lady by the Lake." Because her adult son lived some distance away, she had remembered my offer that she could call on me anytime, day or night.

As our conversation continued, I became aware of the anxiety that dominated her thoughts. The newly prescribed pain medication taken after she had undergone dental surgery had left her feeling dizzy and confused. Her cry for help became my concern, and when I assured her I would be there shortly, she called me her guardian angel. After I told my son our new destination, he no longer regarded ice cream as a priority. How he loved visiting this dear lady!

Because of the urgency to reach her home, the ten-mile trip seemed longer than usual. Thoughts kept reminding me of the perfect timing of her call, and I sensed God's hand guiding me in this journey. When our car began winding around steep curves and rocky cliffs, the small privately-owned lake and her familiar shingled house came into view.

Before my son and I had a chance to knock, we heard a click as she unlocked the door to welcome us. The relieved look on her face already made our trip worthwhile. Once inside, I checked the most recent prescription bottle sitting on the kitchen counter. After talking with her, I felt she had taken the correct dosage. That alone eased my mind. As drowsiness from the medication caused her to want to nap, I waited around until she climbed into bed and then took John home to stay with his dad.

I made several trips back and forth that night, remaining with her through the early morning hours. I tried to nap in her room while I sat in a chair, which certainly didn't compare to my bed, but I felt so thankful her pain and anxiety had finally lessened.

~~~

Remembering past visits at her house brings a smile to my face. Before one such visit, John helped me fill a decorative floral canister with chocolate chip cookies—supposedly her favorite but also his. The three of us soon gathered around her kitchen table ready to have our own little party.

Anticipating the party was almost as much fun as eating, from listening to the fizzling sounds of soft drinks poured over ice to smelling the tantalizing aroma of freshly baked cookies. When John placed the slightly warm cookies on our napkins, a bit of gooey chocolate stuck to his fingers, but he didn't seem to mind. After a brief but thankful prayer, our focus turned to eating cookies.

Although the three of us started with an equal number, a small hand secretly slipped back into the canister for more. As the cookies slowly disappeared, we pretended not to watch. Within minutes, only crumbs remained on our napkins. I then lifted John up to the kitchen sink and balanced him on my knee. I let him turn on the faucet and reach the soap himself to remove all evidence from his hands.

Shortly thereafter, when our friend invited us into her living room to keep her company, John spotted the piano. He awkwardly climbed onto the bench. With reservations, I allowed him to remain but only because of her smiling face and assuring words of approval. Being a first-time experience, his exaggerated movements surprised us all. He raised and lowered his hands high off the keyboard, striking keys randomly as he sang non-sense words.

Her heartfelt laughter became contagious, and John and I found ourselves laughing, too. His comical imitation of a pianist helped ease her sadness, a sadness that accompanied her lost talent, for she remembered the not-so-distant past when she, too, was able to perform, sitting on that same bench. Life returned, if only for a short while, to the usually silent piano.

Another such remembrance might be better if forgotten. When the weather permitted, John and I would follow a slightly worn path in her yard that led down a grassy embankment to an aging boat dock near the water's edge. Although the water usually appeared slightly murky, it remained transparent enough to watch the lively fish darting about, the lucky ones that had escaped the hooks of the local fishermen.

The joy of this event abruptly ended the day we observed snakes slithering about not only in and near the water but also through the tall grassy area along our path. Fish watching became permanently removed from our to-do list. Although we avoided the snakes, we still loved visiting our Lady by the Lake.

~~~

Accepting the changes that age brings to one's life forced our elderly friend to leave her home and relocate in a nursing home closer to her family. Her failing vision and unsteady steps caused concern. Each of our visits revealed the progression of these conditions, which made me realize even more the importance of each trip.

I'll always remember visiting our dear friend for the very last time. Because of the serious condition of her health, the walk down the long hallway filled my heart with sadness. Still holding John's hand, I entered her room. We found her weakened, quietly sitting in a wheelchair near her bed. Because she was almost totally blind, her motionless eyes seemed to be staring across the room. Our physical appearance meant little until she recognized our voices, causing us to reunite in friendship.

Her mind remained quite sharp as we talked about the past and relived happy moments. Near the end of our visit, she shared her disappointment. She could no longer see John, just part of the outline of his body. I asked John to move a little closer to her wheelchair. I guided her fragile hand to the top of his head and helped her to visualize how tall he was. As she lowered her hand and gently felt his face, she sadly remarked, "I wish I could see him just one more time."

Immediately, something unexplainable happened. A look of indescribable peace transformed the expression on her face. She claimed her sight had been restored just long enough to have actually seen John, even though for just a brief glimpse. From the joy that radiated from her face, I believe she received her wish—a gift from a loving and caring God.

As we left her room that day, I was thankful for God's presence and for her love and friendship that had touched my life and John's. I believe God had connected our lives time and time again because of His unconditional love and as an answer to prayer.

Much of what happens in life cannot be fully understood from a human perspective. But I do know this: When God's plans don't coincide with ours, He expects us to act. McDonald's can wait!

CHAPTER ELEVEN

Accepting His Gift

A most humbling gift united the hearts of two strangers in cherished friendship until the unexpected happened.

It was late afternoon. The laughter and noisy chatter of teenagers ended. The shelter in the park was once again quiet. Supervising an after-school outing on such a beautiful day had been quite a contrast from teaching inside a windowless classroom. After I trashed the last of the empty pizza boxes, I was ready to head for home . . . or so I thought.

When I climbed in my car, my heart reminded me of something more—a party I had promised to some forty residents at a personal care facility. I thought to myself, *Tonight? Why tonight?*

No date had been set, but for some unknown reason, I felt it had to be tonight. An unexpected spurt of energy encouraged me to follow my heart. Intent on having this party, I made a quick call to the administration to confirm it. I didn't want to disappoint these people.

Most of these residents struggled with mental issues and past histories of very troublesome lives. They seemed so isolated from the world around them. I often felt they were society's forgotten ones—remembered by God but ignored by people. Throwing a party seemed to inevitably lift their spirits and bring smiles to their distressed faces.

Having little time to spare, I used a mental checklist as I loaded the car with needed items. During the ten-minute drive to this facility, my thoughts switched to their spiritual needs, mainly the prayer before eating. Seldom do I plan the words in advance, but this time I sensed God telling me differently. I was to specifically give thanks for these four things: the beautiful day, our friendship, our food, and most of all, Jesus. No extra words. No flowery phrases. The hope of this prayer was not only to strengthen the faith of believers but also to soften the hearts of nonbelievers.

When I pulled into the parking lot, residents rushed toward the car to help carry in supplies and set up for the party. They knew our routine by heart. A few residents lined up drink cans on the counter, while others removed snack cakes from boxes and sorted ice cream according to flavors. Several volunteered to set bright-colored placements and napkins around on the tables in hopes of giving the dining hall a more party-like atmosphere.

The mention of the word "ice cream" over the intercom ended most early evening naps. Residents hurried to the dining hall from all directions to find their usual seats. Each was handed a cutout with a handwritten message that said: "God Loves You!" That was the theme of our party—in fact, the theme of every party!

As soon as everyone was accounted for, I asked if they were ready to pray. I glanced over the group and found heads bowed in silence, regardless of their beliefs. The prayer was brief as intended. When residents heard the final *amen*, they rushed to get a place in line.

While some were still waiting to select their snacks, I noticed that one of the residents seated at a table directly in front of me finished early and left the room. I didn't know this person, not even his name. But soon he returned, holding something in his hands. The next thing I knew, he offered it to me.

My heart was so moved when I recognized the shape of a cross. As I remembered how little these residents owned, I couldn't bring myself to accept such a gift. Several residents seated around us thought differently, excitedly nodding their heads up and down while repeatedly saying, "Yes, you can!" Although their encouraging response didn't cause me to change my mind, I once again thanked this kind man.

But he wouldn't take no for an answer. Instead, this resident held up his Pepsi can and said, "If I can accept this drink from you, then you have to accept this gift from me!"

Because of the look of sincerity on his face and the convincing tone of his voice, I gave him a hug and accepted his gift—a glass candlestick in the form of Jesus on the cross, symbolic of the greatest Gift ever given! Residents seated around us began clapping. God's presence was undeniable.

Before I left for home, I asked one of the staff members about the man who had given me the cross. "That's Tim," she said.

Humbled by the evening's events, I drove home with tears in my eyes. I repeatedly thanked God for Tim, my newfound friend in Christ, and for the life-changing message of the cross.

As I began my Bible study that evening, I placed the candlestick close by on the kitchen table. My focus kept switching from the words in my Bible to the image of Jesus on the cross. Light reflecting through the glass allowed me to see something more—a painful remembrance of *that* day—a small red dot on the palm of one of His outstretched hands and a thin wavy line on His wrist. I didn't know who, but someone had intentionally added those marks with a red pen as a reminder that, yes, Jesus truly is the awesome sacrifice.

Tim's gift to me—symbolic of the greatest Gift ever given!

A few days later, I returned to the personal care facility so I could visit with Tim. Both of us knew beyond a shadow of a doubt that God had connected our lives in a special way, as brother and sister in Christ. Tim showed me his Bible and three certificates he had earned while in prison. His hunger for God's Word didn't end there. He longed to continue those exact Bible studies and asked for my help.

Not knowing if that would even be possible, I contacted the prison nearly a hundred miles away. I followed their leads. After making several long-distance calls, I was given a local number of a church just a few miles up the road. Although hard to believe, this nearby church that now agreed to sponsor Tim had been his original sponsor while he had been in prison. Hearing that news brought a smile to Tim's face and thankfulness to his heart. Once again, he studied God's Word.

~~~

Less than ten months later, my heart both ached and rejoiced. While I was waiting to pass out snacks to the residents, I mentioned to a staff member that I was headed to Tim's room for one of my usual visits.

She stopped me abruptly and said, "Wait! Haven't you heard?"

By the tone of her voice, I knew something was wrong. My puzzled look caused her to share the sad news. "Tim passed away very suddenly last week."

My first thought was, *No—not Tim!* My heart ached and tears blocked my vision as the realization hit. I couldn't visit with my friend tonight or ever again in this lifetime. Even though I had known him for less than a year, we had shared many thoughts and

Because she was such a petite lady, Mrs. Scherer liked sitting in the same chair with John and the cat, although that became quite a lapful!

CHAPTER TWELVE

The Touch of a Hand

While holding his small hand in mine, I climbed the long flight of wooden stairs time and time again to the house above the garage. Here lived one of the dearest ladies one can only hope to meet in a lifetime.

Soon after the quiet knock on her door, our dear friend graciously greeted my young son and me and invited us into her quaint living room to have a seat. As usual, I chose a cozy spot near one end of her sofa. But John, being two, ignored the invitation and showed more concern over the whereabouts of her furry black cat, better known as Tom.

Immediately he called, "Kitty, Kitty," and intently searched from room to room. Oh, how excited he became when he spotted the cat under the bed! As he crawled on his hands and knees to drag the cat out of hiding, I questioned if friendly feelings of togetherness were mutual.

A floral, winged-back chair became his favorite spot to sit and hold her cat. When it turned on its motor, the purring heard across the room reassured us that all was well with the two of them. And sometimes, the chair held three. Because she was such a petite lady, Mrs. Scherer liked sitting in the same chair with John and the cat, although that became quite a lapful!

Her upcoming ninety-fourth birthday deserved an extra-special

When our dear friend celebrated her ninety-fourth birthday, what made John's gift extra special was the design on the lid—a black cat that looked exactly like hers!

celebration. In the years since her husband had passed, the many friends and acquaintances she made while living in the community and serving in public office had become like family.

One such couple, a pastor and his wife, surprised her with a beautifully decorated cake that was big enough to feed many. They had assumed others would remember her special day and stop by for a visit. Although lots of lovely cards filled her mailbox, she waited all afternoon in anticipation of guests, who knew nothing about the planned celebration. She hid her disappointment well that day and joyfully shared her decorated cake with the thoughtful couple that had furnished it and also a faithful caregiver.

Being on vacation, John and I also missed the celebration. Even though a couple of days late, we still wanted to honor her. So we baked her a cake, frosted it with pink and white icing, and placed John's favorite clown decoration on top. We limited the candles to three instead of the traditional ninety-four—just too many!

After we arrived at her house, she and John stood beside one another next to her cake as we sang "Happy Birthday." Immediately, the two of them combined efforts to blow out the candles, because it was more fun that way. Before we cut the cake, she carefully unwrapped John's gift, a ceramic trinket box. What made it extra special was the design on the lid—a black cat that looked exactly like hers! The pictures taken that afternoon soon became precious memories of a very special friendship.

~~~

In the months that followed, her health became fragile. Because of a past agreement, a lifelong friend promised to carry out her wishes to spend the last hours of her life at home.

One night after dark, something in my heart told me the time was drawing near, and I found myself holding my son's hand to climb those stairs. When we entered the living room, I saw her helplessly lying there in a hospital bed. Compassion for this dear friend filled my heart. I began to wonder how my young son would respond to our loved one so obviously ill, and I questioned my judgment as to whether or not I should have made this last visit alone.

John stood very quietly beside her bed. He wasn't tall enough to see her, except for her frail hand lying near him on top of the sheet. Without saying a word, he reached up with his own little hand and gently patted hers. With her eyes still closed, a slight smile came over her face, and a faint voice sweetly responded, "That's John."

Just like my heart had told me, that night was her last on earth. That small hand would no longer hold mine to climb those stairs again, but his gentle touch seemed to bring an added sense of peace and comfort to our dear friend. God's love was felt that night through the Holy Spirit, the prayers and presence of loved ones, and the touch of a hand.

~~~

Lois Scherer left this earth after a lengthy and meaningful life for a far better place reserved especially for her. She had seemed so appreciative of the life God had given her. Her friendly smile, her soft-spoken voice, and her positive attitude had contributed to making her the dear person we'll never forget.

Regardless of the extreme age difference, she and John shared a mutual bond of love and friendship. Although we only knew her for the last three years of her life, being in her presence had been a real blessing. I recall with fondness her sharing her home, her cat, her lap, her cake, her friendship, her love, and her last night on earth.

In honor of her forty-three years in public office as master commissioner of the county circuit clerk, officials lowered flags to half-staff the morning of her funeral. She had selflessly served her community, fellow human beings, and God.

When I drive past the house located above the garage, I miss climbing those stairs and stopping by for a visit. But I remind myself that this was only her temporary home, and she now enjoys eternal life in the presence of Jesus and fellow believers.

As we live each day, may we too be aware and thankful for His presence, sent perhaps through the touch of a loved one or friend.

CHAPTER THIRTEEN

"Tell God My Name"

Living in one personal care home after another, a lonely and troubled black resident in his early twenties longed to learn how to pray, earnestly seeking a personal relationship with God.

Most residents living at a nearby personal care facility have experienced troublesome lives and tend to be ignored by society. Seldom do they receive a piece of mail from anybody or have a visitor, not even a family member. Much of their day is spent watching television or napping in darkened rooms. Because of their circumstances, fellow residents and a caring staff become like family, as do a few volunteers.

When I began visiting these people, I learned that nothing seemed to get their attention any faster than the word *party*. Regardless of age, they loved having special treats on any day, at any time, and for any reason—or for no reason at all. It didn't matter if it was cold, hot, or rainy outside; inside, a party was always welcomed.

On such days, once the residents found their usual seats in the dining hall, the wait for others tested their patience. Although eager to eat, they would respectfully bow their heads for prayer, regardless of their beliefs. Some professed to be Christians; others confessed they were not. Still others were unsure of what being a

Christian really meant.

One young black resident had acquired a new interest in faith. His name was Dwight. Some days, he seemed to have more questions than I had answers. He asked, "When you pray, what do you say? Where is God? How does He hear?" Because he longed to someday live in heaven, he wanted to know more about this loving God and this thing called prayer.

One evening after a party, Dwight saw that I was leaving and followed me outside to the front of the building—a popular place for residents to hang out. In spite of their presence, he reached out his hands and asked that I pray for him. But prayer was a new experience for him, and as soon as I started to pray, he quickly interrupted by saying, "First, tell God my name."

"Dwight, God already knows your name," I responded. But because of his sincerity and the innocence of such a request, I agreed. When I introduced him by saying, "God, this is Dwight," I bet that caused a bit of amusement in heaven!

With each passing week, Dwight became more inspired to pray. During my visits, he would stop me anywhere—the hallway, the gathering area, the parking lot, and even the dining hall— and reach out his hands for prayer. He didn't care about privacy or location.

Although his faith was increasing, doubt controlled his heart, keeping him distanced from God. He couldn't accept the fact that God actually knew him. Each time before we prayed, he continued to remind me, "Tell God my name again." His tender heart so deeply longed for this personal relationship with God.

Because I wanted him to take a step up in faith, I encouraged him to pray even when alone. Slightly confused, he asked, "What do I say?"

I replied, "Just talk to God like you talk to me."

Months passed. Because of his earnest search through childlike prayers, Dwight discovered a loving God Who knew his name. But things don't always turn out as expected, as I learned in the days that followed.

~~~

One night after snacks, the security light drew attention to a resident pacing back and forth along the side of the building. Even though I had climbed back into my car to leave, my heart signaled me to stay.

I recognized the silhouette of my prayer partner, and even from a distance, I could tell he was troubled. I left my car and headed his direction. I called out to him, asking if things were going okay. I already knew the answer—obviously not.

Dwight unloaded the heavy burden carried in his heart. He knew his acceptance of Jesus assured him of going to heaven, but his heartache was about the recent death of his mom. Aware of her lack of faith, he feared their final destinations would be different and that he would never see her again. Inner turmoil and emotional pain replaced the joy and peace that should have been his. This was a tough realization for him, one I had not anticipated.

The darkness of the night helped Dwight hide his emotions. But in spite of his grief, he held out his hands to pray. He humbly requested of me, "Ask Jesus to take care of my mom." I blinked back the tears, knowing God heard his desperate plea.

Days later, Dwight's actions resulted in a transfer. This was disappointing news in more ways than one. It ended his chance of learning how to read at a nearby facility, and it also distanced us from one another. No staff member could legally tell me his new location, but I found him unexpectedly while I was visiting another personal care home in a town some thirty miles away.

I spent a few minutes talking with him in his room and assumed from our brief conversation that he was adjusting quite well. When I started to back out of my parking space, Dwight came rushing out of the facility, shouting and waving his arms for me to stop. I wondered what was on his mind. When I rolled down my window to talk, he reached out his hands to pray.

~~~

A few months later, I made another trip to the same facility to visit with him. I recognized some familiar faces but not his. Residents informed me that he no longer lived there. I believed they were telling me the truth, but my heart convinced me to do something more—to talk to a nurse's aide, the one busily dispensing medications from a cart at the end of the hallway.

Her face lit up at the mention of his name. She knew him well and assured me of his transfer. When I spoke of Dwight's faith, she showed much concern. At the close of our conversation, I thanked her for the talk.

As I climbed back into my car to leave, she came hurrying out of the building, motioning for me to wait. She had remembered something more that might be of interest to me and began to explain.

Back at the time Dwight lived at that facility, he had sometimes gone to church with her. Regardless of the Sunday, his prayer request had remained the same—just like I had mentioned—for Jesus to take care of his mom. Even more amazing, at a special service where the preacher invited guests to sing, Dwight had volunteered on the spur of the moment, having no music or accompaniment of any kind. She told me how he had stood before the entire congregation—with outstretched hands as if to be holding something—and sang, "He's Got the Whole World in His Hands."

I thought to myself, *Imagine that—going from disbelief and thinking God didn't know his name to glorifying God through song!* His singing and faith must have brought rejoicing in heaven, regardless of the quality of his voice.

Hearing about Dwight's witness increased my desire to see him again. But because no similar facilities were located close to my home, I gave up the search, at least temporarily.

~~~

Several years later, I accompanied my husband on a short business trip to a town some eighty miles away. About halfway there, I thought of Dwight and the possibility of him living in one of their healthcare facilities. My husband agreed to drive me after he had completed his business.

The first two nursing homes I checked were much too lavishly decorated, and even before asking, I knew he didn't live there. But I didn't give up. In fact, one of the nurses I spoke to gave me encouraging news. She described a different type of facility across town that housed people with troubled lives. When I heard the word *troubled*, I became hopeful and thought, *That sounds like Dwight!*

As we headed across town, streets were unfamiliar. I had trouble deciphering the nurse's map. Because my husband had the typical male attitude that you don't stop and ask directions, he drove up and down streets, thinking we would accidentally run into Dwight's place of residence.

But this was a fairly large town. After we had traveled many blocks on a one-way street, I felt we were wasting time and getting nowhere. I couldn't explain why, but I insisted we return to a particular convenient store I remembered seeing earlier. Backtracking such a distance made little to no sense, especially to my husband, but we eventually found the store.

Once inside, I noticed three black people standing near the checkout. Two seemed to be employees; the other, their only customer. They laughed as they talked, greatly enjoying each other's company. When they noticed me, they deliberately paused and asked how they could be of help.

I told them I was looking for a particular personal care facility located nearby. I didn't have to mention the name; they already knew. The customer smiled yet looked quite surprised. "I just came from that place!" he remarked. *Pretty incredible*, I thought to myself. He drew me a simplified map and wrote directions beneath it. I headed out the door thinking, *Too good to be true.*

The concerned customer fell in step with me as I walked back to my car. My ears could hardly believe what they were hearing: *He ministers to the troubled residents at that facility.* Before we parted company, I explained that I, too, had a similar purpose. When he asked if I was looking for someone in particular, I told him, "Yes, his name is Dwight." He couldn't recall the name but offered to check on him during his upcoming visit.

By this time, it was getting quite dark. With the help of the overhead light on the newly sketched map, I navigated while my husband drove. All went well until I didn't say "Turn right" quickly enough, and we missed the turn. When this happened, a car pulled up alongside ours.

The man in that car rolled down the window on the passenger's side to talk and apologized if he in any way frightened us. I should have known; he was the same kind man. He said he lived and worked in that black neighborhood and was quite familiar with the streets. Because we had missed the turn, he said to follow him and he would lead us to our destination. I couldn't help but think, *That sounds like something Jesus would say.*

Even in the darkness of the night, the specialized care center looked similar to what I had imagined. Once inside, I found several residents who knew Dwight. After I checked in with the front desk, the nurse on duty paged his room to tell him he had a visitor. Within minutes, Dwight walked in my direction, wearing a friendly grin.

We greeted each other with a hug, and after a brief conversation, he reached out his hands for prayer. The head nurse at the front desk quieted those around us by saying, "Shh! Shh! They're praying!" Dwight and I parted in opposite directions, certain God would connect our lives again.

~~~

After a time lapse of many months, I needed assurance that God's truth still remained in Dwight's heart. He lived too far for a visit, so I decided to reach him by phone. The wait while the staff located him seemed to take forever.

When he finally answered, he said, "I'm not doing so well but still have the picture of our praying hands." He then asked, "Would you pray for me . . . right now . . . over the phone?"

What a relief—that was all I needed to hear! Prayer remained important to Dwight in his journey of faith, from knowing there is a God to knowing God. Once again, his troubled heart and my grateful heart felt the blessings of answered prayer.

~~~

How amazing that we can turn to God in prayer! Although we don't know exactly how this happens, God Himself hears and answers prayer. He has no busy signals or answering machines. He needs no caller ID. Prayer is powerful. It changes lives, as it did for Dwight and also for me.

As a new believer, Dwight taught me a valuable lesson I hope I will never forget. When a person is the first in a family to accept Jesus, the new Christian not only believes that Jesus is the answer for eternal life but feels concern for other family members who had lived their lives never believing in Christ.

Although constantly tested, real faith is present in Dwight's life. It allows him to understand forgiveness, the cross, and the way to eternal life. He believes God's promises, knowing someday he will live in heaven. Dwight no longer says, "Tell God my name." He is certain God knows.

Reaching out his hands for prayer, Dwight no longer says,
"Tell God my name." He is certain God knows.

The lyrics of a popular praise song titled "He Knows My Name" reminds me of Dwight and of God's love and concern for each of us:

> He knows my name.
> He knows my every thought.
> He sees each tear that falls.
> He hears me when I call.
> —*Tommy Walker*

> *And without faith it is impossible to please God,*
> *because anyone who comes to him must believe that he*
> *exists and that he rewards those who earnestly seek Him.*
> —Hebrews 11:6

CHAPTER FOURTEEN

Late Arrival

Whenever I hear of a flight being delayed, the memory of my friend Francis brings a smile to my heart.

As I drive down the main highway and a local nursing home comes into view, often my heart tugs seem to control the steering wheel of the car, not allowing me to pass by without at least making a quick stop. If I ignore these feelings and continue traveling on down the road, I will find myself on a guilt trip for the rest of the day.

During recent visits to this facility, I faced challenging moments just punching the correct digits on the keypad to gain admittance. Once, when no combination seemed to work, my cell phone came in handy. Through glass doors, I watched a staff member answer my call and look my direction as if to ask, *What's your problem?*

After recovering from a bit of embarrassment, I successfully punched in the code. The light turned green, signaling that the door to the lobby was unlocked. I breathed a sigh of relief but perhaps too soon. As I pushed open the door, an elderly resident tried to sneak out and told me in a most urgent voice of her need to get home.

Once inside the lobby, a confused resident wanted to return to her room and asked for my help. But I didn't know which room was hers. What's worse, she couldn't remember her room number, her hallway, or even her name. A dedicated staff member relieved me of this duty by compassionately taking her hand and leading her back to familiar surroundings.

The lobby was the main gathering place for residents, regardless of their physical condition, and I couldn't help but notice the many looks of loneliness. Saying good morning or giving them an encouraging word or two seemed time well spent. Sometimes just a friendly smile or a loving pat on a shoulder would brighten someone's day, if only for the moment.

Often, I would find my friend Francis sitting quietly in her wheelchair apart from the others, staring blankly across the lobby. Poor eyesight and loss of hearing limited her socializing. I could have easily walked past her without being noticed, but my heart would prompt me to do otherwise.

In order for her to see me, I would squat down beside her wheelchair so my face would be in direct view of hers. I would patiently wait. Seconds later, she would welcome me with her familiar grin and loudly exclaim, "Oh, it's you! I know you!" The way her grin turned into a broad smile would warm anyone's heart. Because she was extremely hard of hearing, if I spoke loudly enough for her to hear, everyone else heard too! We had no private conversations in the lobby or anywhere.

On one particular visit, my eyes scanned the lobby and caught a glimpse of many familiar faces, but I couldn't spot Francis. Because I didn't remember her room number or its exact location, I searched both sides of the hall, glancing from room to room.

Finally, I found her sitting in a wheelchair on the far side of her room with her back toward me, looking out her window. Because I knew she probably wouldn't hear my footsteps and I didn't want to startle her, I walked slowly in her direction, softly calling out her name. With each step, I spoke a little louder. Suddenly, she turned her head and grinned, recognizing my presence.

After we exchanged a few friendly words, curiosity got the best of me. I asked what had caught her attention outside. She replied, "Oh, I'm looking at the beautiful things God has made . . . the trees . . . the clouds . . . the sky." She named things most people don't notice on a daily basis. She was truly enjoying His gifts. Her appreciation of the simple things in life was one of many reasons I found her presence uplifting, and the expression of complacency on her face revealed an inner peace with God.

Later that month, she faced significant health issues. Even with increased oxygen, breathing became quite difficult. Because she felt so badly, she decided the end of her life was near. She persuaded a nurse to call the Catholic priest from the local church to administer the last rites to her. The priest wasted no time carrying out her request, and as he left, she smiled contently and soon fell asleep.

The head nurse said this patient awoke the following morning extremely irritated and disgusted and called the nursing home "a dump!" No wonder she felt disappointed—she thought she would wake up in heaven!

Leaving this earth is according to God's timing, and because God wasn't ready for Francis yet, I was able to stop by to see her one last time. As I quietly peeked into her room, I noticed she was hooked up to numerous monitors and tubes to help prolong her life. I knew my elderly friend was ready and waiting for this life to end so she could move on to a better place. Because we had already said our good-byes, I silently said a little prayer for her as I left her doorway, knowing this godly lady would soon be going home.

~~~

The trip to her final destination wasn't a question of where but when. The Bible assured her that Jesus had prepared a beautiful place in heaven just for her. She greatly anticipated the move to her new home and the faithful she would meet, especially her Savior. Francis thought her delay on earth was much too long, but according to God's timetable, her arrival was perfectly timed.

CHAPTER FIFTEEN

"Just Look Up"

When I stepped outside into the darkness and glanced up at the sky, a star-filled night reminded me of God's presence and the beginning of a friendship never to be forgotten.

The evening party at the personal care facility ended. The trash was emptied, and the doors to the dining hall were once again locked. Residents scattered throughout the facility, but most crowded together in the front lobby to watch television and to talk.

As I pushed open the outside door to leave, the abrupt change from florescent lighting to a star-filled night caught me by surprise. I paused, looking up in amazement. While my eyes scanned the vastness of the darkened sky, my vision continued to sharpen. Numerous twinkling miracles seemed to be popping out from nowhere. "Hey, look at me!" each seemed to shout. A rich, heavenly glow from thousands of stars highlighted the sky in unbelievable brightness.

On the way to my car, I became distracted by yet another unexpected sight. There, in the middle of the parking lot, I noticed an elderly man sitting alone in a wheelchair. That seemed quite unusual, considering the time of night. The security light shining down on his silver-gray hair convinced me I had never seen this gentleman before. Even though he was unknown to me, I felt a great concern for him and started walking in his direction.

I continued to approach his wheelchair, but he didn't seem

the least bit surprised. It was as though he were expecting me. Noticing the sky's intense beauty, this most delightful person who called himself Jack was no less amazed than I. No doubt, the starlit sky had drawn us together, but there was something more. I didn't know why, but something deep down inside was telling me to share my faith with him under this perfect overhead setting.

Throughout our conversation, the brilliance of the sky continued to capture our attention. The full moon and thousands of twinkling stars so illumined the night that even a nonbeliever would have had to take notice. We marveled at their existence, humbled by the mystery and wonder of God's creation. Then, with a stretch of the imagination, our minds allowed us to see something more—billions of stars beyond the earth outside the realm of human sight. Sharing our faith at that moment and giving God the praise and the glory united our hearts in a most powerful way. When I realized the depth of his faith, I knew meeting him was no coincidence.

During the following months, we shared many special moments. We enjoyed each other's company as we talked and laughed, but most likely, it was through the tears and the witnessing and the praying that our friendship significantly strengthened. Several times Jack mentioned to me in confidence, "I just don't feel like I belong here." That remark was true when I compared his life to the lives of other residents, but God seemed to have a unique purpose for his being there.

His caring and compassionate ways not only touched my heart but the hearts and lives of others. He ministered to any resident requesting his help. At times, even the staff sought his sound advice. I considered his wise council a special gift from God and felt privileged to have a friend with such wisdom and faith.

But the reality of life soon hit. Jack began experiencing intense pain and breathing problems related to his lung cancer. Because of the seriousness of this condition, he was rushed by ambulance to a hospital nearly thirty miles away.

Within days, I traveled that same route to pay him a visit. When the elevator abruptly stopped on the fifth floor, I headed straight for Jack's room. I found his door standing partially open and glanced in. There sat my elderly friend with the distinguished gray hair, propped up in bed against several pillows, facing the door as if expecting me. Before I had a chance to say a thing, Jack quickly let me know that he had recognized my silhouette in the doorway and knew who had come to visit even without me speaking.

Inside his room, a professional-looking orderly was finishing his duties and about to leave. I joked with this young man on staff, reminding him to take extra good care of my friend. He assured me he was already doing so. He then glanced over at Jack with a smile, complimenting him for being such a fine person.

When Jack heard that comment, he sat up a little straighter in bed. In his own purposeful way, he began witnessing to him. He reminisced about the night we first met, addressing both the orderly and me. His words went something like this: "You remember—I was sitting outside that night. You know I don't like to be around crowds or a lot of people. It was as if God had said to me, 'Jack, you go outside and look at the stars. I've got someone I want you to meet tonight.' I had not been sitting in the parking lot very long until you came up to me and started talking."

The orderly looked quite puzzled at Jack's words, shaking his head back and forth while commenting, "Strange. Very strange!" Before he left the room, Jack and I assured him it wasn't *strange*, just God's timing. After I visited with Jack a little longer, I prayed with him and left for home.

Within a few days, Jack seemed to be feeling more like his old self. He was transferred back to the personal care facility, but not for long. The seriousness of his health problems caused him to be readmitted to the hospital, and I planned to visit him soon.

When I later arrived at the hospital, the sadness in his eyes and the look of concern on his face told me that something other than his illness was bothering him. He explained that plans were being made to transfer him to a higher-skilled nursing home nearly two hundred miles away. *Two hundred miles away?* I hated to think my usual jump-in-the car, hit-the-road trips of only a few miles would no longer be possible, but I couldn't let him see my disappointment. Because of the progression of his illness, I knew advanced care was a must.

Holding back the tears, I mentioned to Jack that staying in touch could become a bit of a problem. But Jack, unsure of the name and address of his new facility, confidently remarked, "Don't worry about it. God will keep us in touch."

I handed him a gift bag. Inside was Max Lucado's flip calendar, *Grace for the Moment*. I told him that we would be reminded not only of God's presence in our lives but the heart of the other by both of us reading the same message each day.

We continued to reminisce a little about life and reminded one another, "When life gets difficult and we get down in our faith, just look up!" Then Jack, remembering one of his favorite truths, shared again these words: "Without God, there is nothing." I agreed, tucking that thought in my heart for safekeeping. Before I left his bedside, I held his hand for a parting prayer. Our final good-bye was said with a hug.

I deliberately pulled the wide privacy curtain back around

Jack's bed, isolating him from the bright glare of florescent lights, the direct view of others, and most regrettably, my presence. Saying good-bye and walking out that hospital door proved a tender moment in life because of the uncertainty of ever seeing him again.

~~~

Several months passed, but I had not heard from Jack. Because of the worry I felt inside, I decided to search for him. I contacted nursing homes, tried to locate possible relatives, and visited a veteran's hospital some ninety miles away. Staff members at that facility searched computer records and called affiliated nursing homes to find out if he were still living, but there was still no trace of Jack. In spite of my efforts, I accomplished little to nothing. I didn't know what else to do. I impatiently waited. I wanted the hurt of not knowing his whereabouts to go away. Days turned into weeks.

After I returned home from a weekend trip, I noticed the blinking red light on my answering machine. I hit the play button and heard the recorded message: "This is Jack. Remember? The one you knew at the home? You aren't at home, but if I get another chance, I'll call you again." The sound of his voice helped restore peace to my heart.

But regardless of the number of times I replayed his message, there was no trace of a phone number, no mention of an address, not even a hint of his whereabouts. I never found Jack, but hearing his voice for that very last time was an answer to my prayer.

I believe God took him home before he had another chance to call. I no longer worry and wonder where Jack is. I know where he lives; he lives in the presence of God. I know the condition of his health; he's perfectly healed. I know he's not lonely or afraid; he's in good company with Jesus and fellow believers.

~~~

When problems overwhelm me and doubts rob my heart of faith, I go outside many a night and glance up at the sky. Whether it's fair or cloudy, stars or no stars, my thoughts turn to Jack and the star-filled night when the Holy Spirit united us in everlasting friendship.

Like Jack assured me during my last visit while he lay critically ill in the hospital, "God will keep us in touch." And so He has, not only through the use of an answering machine but also by revealing His glory on a star-filled night. I can still hear Jack saying, "Just look up!"

Knowing my husband's tractor once belonged to her late husband, Ruby would amusingly ask, "How's the tractor?"

late husband was already there, impatiently waiting for her and the chance to ask, "Ruby, what took you so long?"

Her comment left me feeling a bit amused, but not for long. After she shared those thoughts, sadness filled her heart, and she broke down crying. She confessed that she had forgotten the words to the Lord's Prayer and the Twenty-third Psalm. I told her we'd say that prayer together, and so we did. Then she worried about remembering the words when I wasn't there. To help ease her mind, I printed the prayer and scripture in extremely large letters and placed them inside the front of her Bible. Having a relationship with God was important to her.

~~~

During her final days, she ate so little and seldom opened her eyes. I felt so helpless as she endured the pain and impatiently waited for death. Because of the seriousness of her illness, a "No Visitors" sign was placed on her door. The staff at the nurses' station told me I could ignore it but that she was no longer responding to anyone. Regardless of how difficult, I knew I had to tell her a final good-bye.

When I sadly entered the room and saw her frail body and closed eyes, I felt certain this visit would be my last. As I softly called out her name and told her mine, she wiggled her fingers. I knew that was her good-bye. Mixed emotions filled my heart. After I prayed for her at her bedside, I gave her a final kiss on her cheek and left as quietly as I had entered.

Very soon, the wait was over. No longer would I be asked, "How's the tractor?" No longer were Ruby and her husband impatiently waiting.

CHAPTER SEVENTEEN

Fireworks, Forgiveness and Freedom

Residents at a nearby personal care facility excitedly watched the Fourth of July fireworks light up the sky, while a veteran, sitting in their midst, desperately searched for forgiveness and freedom.

After a quick cleanup following the evening snack in the dining hall, I joined the residents outside who were anxiously waiting for darkness and the highlight of the day's celebration. As the staff carefully lit the mysterious cardboard cylinders and cone-shaped objects on the blacktopped parking lot, everyone's eyes turned upward in anticipation. Countless, unpredictable colorful flashes lit up the darkened sky, accompanied by loud sizzles and bangs that interrupted the usual quiet of the late evening hours.

Glimpses of happiness camouflaged troubled lives when many residents, including several seated in wheelchairs, chose to join in the fun. As soon as their handheld sparklers were ignited, they waved them aimlessly to and fro, which left overlapping trails of glittering light and dense smoke hanging briefly in the air.

The intense noise from the fireworks made it impossible to carry on a personal conversation with anyone. But as soon as the fireworks ended, I immediately felt drawn to a new resident still sitting in his wheelchair in the middle of the parking lot, rather isolated from everyone else.

When close enough to speak, I casually mentioned to Gary that the weak batteries in my camera prevented me from taking Fourth of July pictures as I had in the past. Somewhat disappointed, he asked if I might take his picture at a future date. He told me about wanting photos for family members. And then, with a bit of sorrow, he added, "And relatively soon, because I don't feel I'll be living as long as Christmas."

Just the thought—*not living until Christmas*—replayed over and over in my mind. He started to explain the reason for making such a statement, but after he named several serious health issues, he paused and removed a paper from his wallet. He unfolded it and handed it to me, hoping to make his health status easier to understand. Sure enough, this letter from the Veterans Administration stated proof of his diagnosis in black and white: bone cancer, diabetes, degenerative bone disease, asthma, and hepatitis C.

As I stood beside his wheelchair, my heart felt his despair. I sensed God had purposely arranged our connection that night. It seemed as though this resident desperately needed a friend, someone to talk to. I didn't know why, but I felt the need to write down his thoughts. Gary spoke slowly, especially when tears blurred my vision, as he shared:

> I know I am dying. I don't have long to live. I think about Jesus every day. I came from a Christian family. I guess they gave up on me. I used to be dragged to church. I didn't want to go. I don't know why. I just didn't want to go.
>
> I just turned sixty last month, and I can never remember being happy in my whole life. I don't know what real happiness is. Even though I know that Jesus died on the cross for my sins, most likely, I am going to hell in that I

don't have faith about forgiveness—the hard part.

Every night I go to bed, I think this might be my last. If something like chemo or radiation would stop or slow this cancer down by some miracle, I would have faith. I always thought I would be a great witness for the Lord.

I could give testimonies about the war that would shock people. No one could ever forgive me. I can never forgive myself. If I can never forgive myself, how can I expect a powerful Lord to forgive me?

I know what I have to do to be a Christian. I have no problem believing about Jesus dying for me. In fact, I would love more than anything in life to be a true Christian.

I've tried to ask the Lord to come into my life many times. The only problem is getting up off my knees and thinking that I have a new slate in life, but the feeling is the same. Even though I pray, when I am done, it's like I've never prayed at all. I need to forgive myself, but I can't do it. I believe Satan is pushing me not to forgive or forget the things I've done.

I'd love to be happy, but what defines happiness? I think that happiness is different for every human being. I think happiness is being a Christian, and all Christians have one thing in common—they know they are going to a happy place.

My mother was so happy when we went to see her in the hospital. I was crying because I loved her so much. She said she was going to be with Jesus, and that made her not afraid of dying. She welcomed it. She knew she would see her children again someday. I am so ashamed to let people see me cry. I go to my room, but my roommate sometimes listens to me moan and groan and cry all night.

Both Gary and I considered his health issues overwhelming and life-threatening. And what seemed to me far more disturbing than health issues was his confession that he felt he would never be forgiven.

Gary's request to have his picture taken was not forgotten. He imagined looking best in a dark blue shirt and matching tie.

Days later, those wishes came true. My son brought home his professional camera, and we paid Gary a visit.

~ ~ ~

The timing in God's plan was unlike our fear. Despite his many illnesses, Gary lived long after Christmas. It wasn't until a couple of years later that he faced medical problems that mandated his transfer to a VA hospital several hours away. Unaware of his leaving, I failed to say good-bye. Somehow, as time passed on, the remembrance of this bothered me. I tried to contact him by phone and mail, but regardless of my efforts, I received no response.

One night as I began to worry, my heart reminded me to pray. After I fell asleep for hours, I suddenly awoke, sensing God had plans for me. His voice wasn't audible to my ears, only to my heart. Being the early morning hours, I felt God asking me to visit Gary that very same day. I questioned, *This very day?* My heart received the answer—*Why bother to pray if not willing to obey.* I continued to listen.

I was to deliver a message to Gary to assure him he would be a great witness for the Lord. Most importantly, I was to remind him that God, too, had watched the innocent die: He had sent His Son to die for him. I felt I was to ask permission from the chaplain at the VA hospital to share copies of Gary's story with other patients. I then realized, *What a perfect audience!* Right in his midst were more than a hundred fellow veterans, many of whom were experiencing similar postwar syndrome. Even with those thoughts racing through my mind, I managed to fall back asleep.

When I awoke at seven o'clock to the sound of my alarm, I turned on my usual televised church service and started listening to a message relating to obedience. But when my focus switched to Gary, I began to doubt: *What if my friend doesn't acknowledge me after traveling such a distance? What if I have this all wrong?* Minutes later, the preacher explained that if you follow what your heart feels is obedience and things don't turn out like you expect, God will turn it around for His good. Hearing that message confirmed my feeling that I should pay Gary a visit that day.

Even though it was a Sunday, I decided to miss church and hit the road. Plans worked out to team up with my husband as driver and to meet up with my son as photographer. Before I left, I grabbed my copy of Max Lucado's *Grace for the Moment*, an *In Touch* magazine, and a blanket I had received from the Disabled Veteran's National Foundation with white embroidered words, "FREEDOM IS NOT FREE."

Anxious moments preceded my visit as I considered my friend's privacy and my unannounced presence. But when I knocked on his door and heard his favorable response, I was convinced of a plan far greater than my own.

As Gary glanced at the size of the patriotic gift bag I was holding, he boldly asked, "Did you bring me a book?" I explained that it was my personal copy of a favorite daily devotional and offered it to him. Before I placed it on his bedside table, I flipped the pages to the present date and read Max Lucado's spiritual message entitled, "Adopted by God." I should have known it would relate to forgiveness. It explained that God does more than just forgive us. He gives us His name, and we become His children. What a comforting thought to remember!

I explained to Gary the reason for my visit and the possibility of sharing his story with fellow veterans. He seemed pleased, and after I spoke with the nurse and chaplain, we joined hands with Gary in prayer, aware of the presence of a loving and forgiving God.

After my son and I received permission to take a picture in his room, we unfolded the burgundy blanket and draped it across Gary's chest as he rested his hands above and below the motto. When finished, he proudly claimed ownership of the blanket, which I folded and placed over the back of his wheelchair. Gary remarked, "I'll fix it later." I knew that meant placing the motto, *Freedom is not free*, so all could see when he maneuvered his wheelchair up and down the hallways.

The chaplain approved the plan for sharing Gary's story about forgiveness, along with treat bags and thank-you's, with the hundred or so veterans who were patients there. He considered my offer to deliver it the week of Valentine's Day perfectly timed. He mentioned that the facility would receive numerous cards that week—a week officially known as *National Loyalty Week for Hospitalized Veterans*. I had never heard of such a week and realized immediately it was God's perfect timing.

On the following Sunday when my husband and I made the delivery, I was surprised to hear that Gary was no longer a patient. He had been dismissed earlier in the week. I knew administration couldn't tell me his whereabouts because of privacy law, but I remembered a town he had mentioned during my previous visit. Although I looked, I was never able to find him.

Wherever Gary might be living, my hope is that he is experiencing the true freedom he had longed for by accepting God's forgiveness in his heart. Somehow, perhaps even through the sharing of this story, I pray that Gary will be a great witness for the Lord. It seems a miracle that he is still alive despite the devastating health issues that I read in his VA letter of diagnosis. Only God knows the purpose.

~~~

This blanket, draped across the chest of a veteran in a VA hospital, says it all.

Freedom—many have fought for it physically, mentally, emotionally, and spiritually. The papers from the Veterans Administration do not mention the pain and the emotional scars left on the hearts of those carrying out orders, especially during times of war. Nor do X-rays show the guilt trapped inside the body that leaves a spiritual life disconnected from its Power Source, making a person feel unworthy.

The battle may rage on in a person's anguished mind long after active duty is ended. Reliving the past may destroy the feeling of forgiveness. God knows the dedication and trials of those who serve their country, especially during times of war, and wants to rescue those paralyzed from such feelings of unforgiveness. God's plan: the cross.

CHAPTER EIGHTEEN

Cruisin' in a Wheelchair

The guest speaker confidently wheeled herself across the gym floor toward the podium. As she was handed the microphone, a solemn hush fell over the entire audience of both students and faculty. Her message touched the hearts of many, including mine.

About five hundred high school students sat crowded together on hard metal bleachers on one side of the slightly darkened gymnasium, waiting for the midmorning assembly program regarding safety and trauma prevention. By the looks on their faces, they didn't seem the least bit disappointed for having to skip a class or two, but missing lunch would have been an entirely different matter!

After the principal's brief introduction of the guest speaker, the student body politely applauded as an attractive young lady named LaDonna confidently wheeled herself across the polished gym floor. All eyes focused on her, and with microphone in hand, she courageously and emotionally began sharing her story:

"On January 9, 1995, I was leaving for work and carrying a handgun under my arm with the intention of going to a shooting range after work. When I sat down in the car, the gun fell and hit the car or pavement, discharging a bullet through my kidney and spine. I was immediately and permanently paralyzed from the waist down."

As LaDonna relived this devastating accident in her mind, she fought hard to hold back the tears. But in spite of her efforts, a few managed to escape. A feeling of compassion for this hurting person swept over the audience. Besides her soft-spoken voice, no hint of talking or whispering could be heard throughout the packed bleachers, not even during brief moments of silence.

Students continued to listen attentively as she warned them about the careless use of handguns—the mistake that cost her the use of her legs in the prime of life. Giving the presentation from the seat of a wheelchair offered living proof as to the validity of her warning. After she responded openly and honestly to student questions following her speech, a warm and sincere applause echoed throughout the gym as a few wiped tears from their eyes. Hopefully, her intended message would help all listeners avoid similar devastating experiences.

LaDonna's speech proved to be much more than just a safety issue with guns. She inspired those in attendance to persevere when facing extreme hardships in life, like the times we want to cry out, "Not fair," even though the circumstances don't change. Hidden within her message was evidence of faith, her source of inner strength, which helped her fight the daily battles in life.

Because the student body appeared quite touched by her presentation, I changed my lesson plans for the rest of the day. During the ten-minute break following the assembly, I thanked her, copied her mailing address, and made a quick trip home less than a mile away. I hurriedly gathered an assortment of note cards and decorative computer paper before I rushed back to school.

Back in the classroom, instead of doing the usual computer assignment, the students chose to correspond with the guest speaker. I assured them that envelopes would be sealed and

LaDonna claimed the cards from students were like "repeated hugs from God."

messages would remain private. When students combined artistic ability with writing and computer skills to accomplish their visions, enthusiasm became contagious and creativity emerged.

Intermingled in the regular classroom were students with special needs. They wrote notes and drew pictures the best they could. To add finishing touches, they chose to decorate their work with stickers—actually, lots and lots of stickers—thinking the more the better. I tended to agree.

One by one, students formed a line by my desk to share with me their finished work. The expressions on their faces said it all. I knew their kind words of encouragement would be a blessing to LaDonna. A senior football player even requested an extra day to complete his card, needing to finish a detailed drawing of praying hands. Her gift bag became stuffed with notes of thanks and compassionate messages. Before I mailed this package, I added a personal note and enclosed a book of daily devotional readings, *Grace for the Moment*.

Days later, a thank-you note arrived in my mailbox at school. In part, here is the message:

> My words cannot express the joy that your cards and book have brought since their arrival. It has truly been like repeated hugs from God as you've shared your feelings with me and given encouragement. I pray you'll each cherish what you got from our time together and have a safe and joyful summer! Many thanks!

She also shared with me some personal issues and remarked how the devotional book had been so fitting. Reflecting on the book, she wrote, "It is that grace from God, even if just for the moment, that gets us through."

Whether cruisin' in a wheelchair on a dream vacation or along the daily paths of life, LaDonna truly is a humble and remarkable servant of God.

Months later I received an unexpected postcard in the mail. It pictured a luxurious cruise ship docked off the shoreline of a beautiful resort town in Mexico. My first thought was, *Who do I know enjoying such a vacation?* To my surprise, the card was signed "LaDonna."

She told of the "awesome" seven-day cruise she had earned through her business. As I read on, she mentioned the daily devotional book she had taken with her and its timely messages. "There have been so many days that it has given me the grace needed for the day." In closing, she commented, "I agree that God puts people in your life." Her postcard and caring remarks strengthened our friendship. Imagining my special friend cruisin' in a wheelchair brought a smile to my face.

Recently, my friend climbed aboard another luxury liner, but this time she had earned an Alaskan cruise. Once again, LaDonna's perseverance and hard work had paid off.

~~~

Whether LaDonna is cruisin' in a wheelchair facing daily challenges, sharing her message with young people about making smart choices in life, selling products in her line of business, or enjoying a leisurely vacation on a luxury liner, she truly is a humble and remarkable servant of God. Regardless of circumstances, she believes His grace is sufficient. She is most willing to give her testimony wherever she is called, and she considers it a privilege to do so for His glory.

Now and then a card or e-mail or perhaps a phone call keeps

us in touch. But we feel certain it is through God's love that we are truly connected in friendship. Her e-mail address—bywheelzigo—suggests her upbeat attitude.

No doubt that being confined to a wheelchair makes life much more difficult. But God does not expect LaDonna to live each day in her own strength but in His. The scripture "The joy of the Lord is your strength" (Nehemiah 8:10) is evident in her life.

You, too, can receive His grace and strength and His promise of eternal life. Like LaDonna, regardless of the circumstances, just keep on believing and sharing His love.

When people ask if she'll ever walk again, LaDonna typically responds, "I'll walk again on the streets of gold in heaven, and it can't get better than that!"

CHAPTER NINETEEN

Amazing Grace

A bullet changed his life, and so did God.

As a friend and I walked past the designated smoking area at a local personal care facility, the cigarette smoke that lingered in the air reminded me of early morning fog in the mountains. The unattractive concrete walls of this small, boxed-in area were unevenly lined with unmatched, worn-out chairs and tobacco-stained smoking stands. Residents were seated randomly, taking advantage of their midmorning smoking break.

In the midst of this smoke, a friendly middle-aged black man who was seated in a wheelchair introduced himself as Keith and offered to sing "Amazing Grace" for us. He was so intent on singing that the tug at my heart to listen overpowered my doctor's orders to avoid all smoke-filled areas.

When the sound of his voice filled the air, his God-given talent was obvious. He used no CD, no tape, no music or accompaniment of any kind. He relied only on his voice, an incredibly beautiful voice, as he humbly sang about God's love and His amazing grace.

Without a doubt, his singing was worthy of an audience—an earthly one in addition to a heavenly one. Although the spiritual part of me longed to stay, the physical part of me needed a breath of fresh air. But without pause, the end of one song transitioned into another, leaving us no time to properly thank him and exit this smoke-filled room.

As I tried not to inhale too deeply, I remained with my friend, listening to yet another song titled "Sanctuary." With eyes nearly closed, this Spirit-filled Christian poured out his heart to God. He sang the words, "Let me be your sanctuary," with sincerity.

What a spiritual boost his singing had been in the middle of an ordinary morning! The physical disability that confined Keith to a wheelchair certainly didn't diminish his ability for sharing God's love. I left for home, aware that Keith's singing was part of God's plan and that our paths would cross again.

Days later, when Keith painfully shared the cause of his paralysis with me, he blamed only himself. During his teenage years, he had become involved in gang violence in a largely populated city in Kentucky. During a drive-by shooting, a bullet had lodged in his spine, leaving him paralyzed in both legs and one arm. Because of the dangerous location of the bullet, surgery had not been an option, and no amount of therapy could relieve his condition.

In spite of his infirmity and confinement to a wheelchair, Keith stayed busy and useful in life, praising God through it all. When the weather allowed him no choice but to remain inside, he spent countless hours rearranging items in his room and cleaning the floor. Mopping from the seat of a wheelchair with the use of his one functioning arm was a physical challenge. But he refused help, wanting to accomplish this task through his own perseverance.

Keith didn't stay confined to the grounds of that facility. Motorists traveling up and down the main highway as I often did could see him picking up trash and sacking it from his wheelchair. The red bandana tied around his forehead and the American flag attached to the back of his wheelchair easily identified him. Such community service was not uncommon for Keith. He seemed to enjoy it along with the freedom of being outdoors.

His wheelchair didn't represent a seat for a handicapped person but mobility for a Christian ready and willing to serve his Lord. Keith's ministry of praise and song extended to neighboring churches, whose members gladly went out of their way to transport him to and from their special services. The outpouring of their love left an impact on Keith's heart.

His singing was a precious gift from God, a blessing to all who heard. He never sang to attract personal attention but rather to humbly share his love of Jesus. My faith increased when he sang and prayed at the end of each of my visits.

Keith knew where the light at the end of his life would lead him. Even though his faith was constantly tested, God remained his source of joy and strength. His singing, his prayers, his witness, and his life all glorified God.

Later he was diagnosed with additional health problems, including diabetes. He found adjusting to that lifestyle quite difficult. For months, he chose not to sing publicly, which left a void in his heart.

~ ~ ~

One Sunday afternoon, I felt a sense of urgency to check on him. While I talked with him outside, I realized how very restless and troubled he had become. I didn't know exactly what his heart was feeling, but mine told me to encourage him to sing.

Because I wanted Keith to have an audience of more than one, I asked if he would sing "Amazing Grace" for a spiritual friend of mine. Keith agreed, and I made a call. Regardless of the inconvenience, my friend not only stopped what he was doing but also brought another. Although unaware, the two of them became an answer to a prayer.

Keith's wheelchair didn't represent a seat for a handicapped person but mobility for a Christian ready and willing to serve his Lord.

Keith knew where the light at the end of his life would lead him.

Even though it was a hot and sunny afternoon, the three of us stood under a shade tree beside Keith's wheelchair, listening to his humble voice over the passing motorists and the chirping birds. Usually, he sang only two or three songs, but today seemed more like a special concert. He sang song after song after song. His voice and his heart belong to an incredible servant of God.

Before we left, the four of us joined hands the best we could despite his paralysis, and Keith led us in a prayer. Hearing such praise and devotion from the seat of a wheelchair while sensing God's powerful presence united our hearts in humble devotion.

Three days later I understood the urgency to hear Keith sing. He had left the facility quietly, without good-byes. That had been his final concert for me. Privacy law prevented disclosure of his new location. I knew his transfer to a skilled nursing home had been a positive move, but I already missed him.

~~~

About six months had passed, but I still knew nothing of Keith's whereabouts. I wanted so badly to be able to thank him and to share the photos my son had taken. Administration agreed to address and to mail my package. Hoping to hear back from him, I enclosed a self-addressed, stamped envelope and a small sheet of paper. Because of the paralysis of his right hand, I added a note asking that a caregiver at his new facility write a quick line or two to ease my mind and to let me know he was doing okay.

Months later, there was still no word from Keith. I became quite concerned. I didn't know what else to do. I doubted if I would ever hear from him again.

One day at school, I felt rather sad, remembering that particular day would have been my mother's eighty-ninth birthday.

It was my first year without her, and I greatly missed her. Because I lived close by, I decided to make a quick trip to the comfort of my home during my lunch break.

Out of habit, I stopped at the mailbox. Tucked between other pieces of mail, a letter was addressed to me in my own handwriting. When I saw the return address, I could hardly wait to open it.

The message read, "It was so good to hear from you. I am president of the resident council and still keeping up the faith and prayers. I'm getting along well. I'm visiting church and having homebound Bible discussions. May the Lord bless you! Good hearing from you!"

At the close of this dictated letter, someone signed Keith's name and wrote his last remark, "Will always love ya." After I read his letter for the second time, I thought, *Yes, Keith, I'll always love you, too!*

Receiving Keith's letter on what would have been my mom's special day filled part of that empty place in my heart with love. I recalled the many times she had tied the "God loves you" messages on his little gifts as well as the gifts of others. I was so thankful for the perfect timing of his letter and being able to stay in touch. When Keith later relocated, he remembered to send me his new address.

~~~

One Sunday afternoon, nearly two years after I had last seen Keith, my family agreed to make the seventy-mile trip to his new place of residence. As we drove into the entrance of this beautifully landscaped facility, I breathed a sigh of relief and whispered a prayer of thanks, never imagining Keith to have such a fine earthly home.

Keith humbly praised God through song and prayer.

Once inside, I headed straight for his room. The unannounced visit made my heart beat a little faster. With his door standing wide open, one glance confirmed his presence. Because he lay on his bed facing the opposite direction, he didn't see me standing there. I quietly knocked on the facing of his door, anxious for a response.

He hollered out, "Come on in!" while slowly but deliberately swinging his body around on the bed to see who was there. Immediately, he recognized me. Our hearts filled with joy. His new life was obviously agreeing with him. He not only looked younger in years, but his health seemed much improved.

We spent much time reminiscing, recalling times of sadness as well as times of joy. During a pause in conversation, Keith proudly handed me one of his personal business cards that identified his new leadership position: *Resident Council President.* Among other duties, he was in charge of greeting guests. But the best news was yet to come. He assured me of his continued witness and agreed to another private concert before my leaving.

Prior to wheeling himself out the double doors to the front lawn, a nurse tied a red bandana around his forehead. Once outside, he humbly praised God through song and prayer. His surroundings had changed, but it was evident Keith's heart had remained the same.

The Holy Spirit continues to unite our hearts in friendship, allowing me to be blessed by the purity and conviction of his faith. In the best of times and in the worst of times, our hearts remain hopeful because of God's promise of eternal life and His amazing grace!

CHAPTER TWENTY

Lifting the Mask

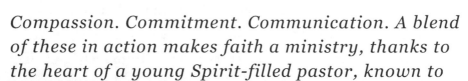

Compassion. Commitment. Communication. A blend of these in action makes faith a ministry, thanks to the heart of a young Spirit-filled pastor, known to many as Brother Jeff.

It was two o'clock on a bright and sunny afternoon, time for the Sunday worship service to begin in the dining hall of a nearby nursing home. This was more than a get-it-over-with, fulfill-our-obligation service. It was an outpouring of God's love to those people and a concern for their faith and salvation.

The invitation given to the residents as we stopped by each room before the service was simply to come. But to come wasn't always easy. It took the joint effort of a caring staff and family members along with a church ministry team to transfer residents to the dining hall.

Very few were able to walk independently. Many needed the assistance of a steadying arm or walker. Some residents wheeled themselves, but most needed someone to push them, especially if their care required the use of oxygen. Still others wanted to attend, but sickness and pain confined them to their rooms.

As Brother Jeff began the service by welcoming the residents, most conversations came to an end. But one elderly lady who was loudly sharing remembrances of the past continued to do so. Another lady had nodded off to sleep. In spite of multiple distractions, the service continued. The preacher announced the first song to be sung.

How those residents loved music! Making songbooks with large print made poor eyesight less of a problem. A songbook held upside down or a page number not found was met with quick assistance. Faces lit up as they recognized familiar hymns. Whether the residents could carry a tune or not didn't really matter. Whether they sang loudly or softly or not at all, that didn't matter either. All that really mattered was their heartfelt connection with Jesus.

Near the end of the singing, the pastor asked for special requests. A soft-spoken lady, quite advanced in years and totally blind, asked that we sing her favorite song, "Jesus Loves Me." By the sweet expression of contentment on her face, she knew this to be true. She loved singing this song, because it brought back memories of childhood days.

After the pastor prayed and shared a brief but timely message, communion was served to those who wished to partake. What concerned me were the bedridden patients who wanted to come but were too weak and too ill to be transported from their rooms. I quietly slipped out of the dining hall in search of those residents.

My heart reminded me of a private room where a man lay critically ill. Day after day, his wife remained at his bedside as his condition worsened. Because I had stopped by this room several times in the past, I felt connected to this couple without actually knowing them.

I quietly tapped on his open door before I stepped inside the room. I didn't know if they belonged to any particular church, but I told them of our pastor's willingness to serve communion at his bedside if he so wished. The wife graciously accepted the offer. Despite the husband's grave condition, he gave a slight nod in agreement.

As soon as the service ended in the dining hall, the pastor came to the patient's room, aware that this celebration of the Lord's Supper might be his last. As he leaned over at his bedside, Brother Jeff slightly elevated the patient's head with one hand while he briefly lifted the man's oxygen mask with the other. As he placed the consecrated elements to the man's lips, he repeated Jesus' words: "Do this in remembrance of me." The brief lifting of the oxygen mask that helped sustain his earthly life allowed him to partake of communion in remembrance of Jesus, his hope for eternal life.

On my next visit to that facility, I looked into his room, but he was not there. I knew he was living in a far better place, free of oxygen masks and pain as promised in God's Word. I slowly walked on by, thanking God for eternal life and for Brother Jeff's humbling act of obedience.

~~~

Several years later, Brother Jeff was asked to serve another church some distance away. The thought of his family leaving nearly broke my heart. I remembered his support and encouraging words in some of the most devastating times of my life. He was there for me during a hospital stay. He was the one I phoned when I found myself in a hospital hundreds of miles from home at the bedside of a sister who had no chance of surviving. His words of comfort and suggested passages of scripture still help me cope in times of grief.

Another remembrance was the day Brother Jeff showed up at the high school after he heard about the tragic death of one of our students. This young person, an outstanding student and track star, had been killed in an accident early one Saturday morning on his way to catch the school bus. Everyone who knew him well knew he had a heart for God. But inside my classroom, the empty chair beside the unused computer seemed too much to bear. Brother Jeff had just returned from the East Coast after he had been preaching his own father's funeral. That pain was still fresh on his heart, but he spent the entire school day helping us deal with our grief. He gave hugs. He prayed, and he counseled. Some of the students claimed they would have never made it through the day without him. I felt the same.

I also remembered when he taught a special class for youth, which led to my son and others making personal commitments to God and becoming members of the church. While he spent most of his time teaching them biblical truth, he had reserved a little one-on-one time following their sessions to teach how to put a bit of a spin on a ping-pong ball.

~~~

The week of Brother Jeff's move, I often found myself at the parsonage, longing to spend more time with this family. I offered to help them pack and became involved in routine chores. I remember sitting on the living room floor with their two young daughters, tossing the laundered clothes, which I was supposed to be folding, on top of their little heads and listening to them giggle. Hearing the laughter helped ease the pain of their leaving.

The family's final hours at the parsonage arrived much too quickly. In the process of boxing up the last of their items, they paused a moment and shared their wedding album before they packed it. The last of the challenging jobs that evening was to

The fortieth birthday party had been kept a secret, greatly surprising Brother Jeff, and a surprise also awaited his guests.

round up the cats, which weren't especially cooperative. Finding them in the dark wasn't easy.

When the door to the parsonage was finally locked and the children and cats were safely loaded into the vehicle, I didn't want to say good-bye. I gave each family member and then Brother Jeff a hug. He made it easier by saying, "We won't say good-bye—just see you later." As they pulled out of their driveway for the last time, his parting words helped convince my heart that our paths would someday cross again.

~~~

Within the next several years, my husband and I traveled some distance to sit in his congregation to again hear him preach. Afterward, we joined others and visited with him and his family during a leisurely meal at a restaurant. It was a lovely afternoon, but nothing compared to the evening of his fortieth birthday.

Prior to this day, an invitation had arrived in the mail from his church family. It told of a surprise party to be held at a convention center over a hundred miles away. We arrived early. When we entered the banquet room, we were greatly surprised by elaborate decorations with a definite Elvis theme. Everywhere I looked, there were life-size cutouts of Elvis and colorful remembrances from that era. The party had been kept a secret, which greatly surprised Brother Jeff, and there was also a surprise awaiting his guests.

The food was delicious and plentiful. After everyone had finished eating, Brother Jeff left our company for a short while. On his return, the room echoed with roars of laughter. He wore a thick wig of unruly black hair that tapered down into long sideburns. Glittering sequins and rhinestones accented his shiny white outfit.

finding two medium shirts that buttoned up the front would be no problem. I checked shirt after shirt for size and wear, scooting the wire hangers down the metal rack as we rejected each garment. After I examined the last shirt, the realization hit—there were no suitable medium shirts!

At this point, I hoped God wouldn't mind my stretching the truth a bit. I told this man that I knew someone giving away medium-sized, button-up-the-front shirts, just the kind he wanted. The word *free* sounded good to him!

After he introduced himself as Sherman Deal, he told me his local address. Although he didn't want me to pay postage, he left the choice of mailing the shirts or delivering them up to me. He repeatedly thanked me in advance.

With great effort and the help of a cane, he painfully moved his body to the next section. My eyes followed, watching in amazement. His stooped condition limited his vision to items sitting on the floor and beneath the tables, never any higher.

As he slowly maneuvered his body from item to item, I pretended to shop beside him and offered my help. Out of politeness, he commented that he really needed nothing but just enjoyed looking. Watching him enjoy life with his limited physical ability made me stop and think, *That kind of joy and perseverance only comes from God.*

Because Mr. Deal seemed to have traveled there alone, I asked if he had family. His explanation of why he never married exposed the kindness of his heart. For twenty years, he had cared for his dad, who had suffered a head injury after a fall. I thought, *What a loving son, placing this burden on himself in the prime of life.* Though the size of his shirt was only a medium, the size of his heart was extra-large.

I asked if he had transportation home. He explained that he had driven his car and lived just blocks away. I couldn't quite imagine him driving, but I knew he was telling the truth. After I reassured him that he would receive two free shirts, I said good-bye and turned to leave, realizing the special blessing placed in my path.

I soon found myself in the men's clothing department at a store in the mall, buying two medium shirts in colorful plaids that seemed perfect for Mr. Deal. Before mailing these shirts, I removed the plastic bags, pins, tags, and cardboard—evidence of their recent purchase. I unbuttoned and refolded them along with a black cardigan sweater, trying to give them a secondhand look.

As the weeks passed, I wondered if the shirts fit. A phone call one evening assured me that he had received the package but had not yet opened it. He told me his arthritis was acting up a little but that he planned to get the shirts out soon. Once again, he expressed thankfulness not only for the shirts but also for God and our friendship.

I felt certain he would be wearing one of those new shirts on Thanksgiving, but another call told me my assumption was wrong! He had opened his Thanksgiving card but still not the package. I began to wonder.

A day or two after Christmas, a phone call confirmed the truth: Because he lived alone, he admitted saving that package for his Christmas. Now that he had opened it, when his family members stopped by during the holidays, he loved showing them his shirts.

During the cold and lonely days of winter, we kept connected through phone calls, mail, and prayer. Hearing his voice or receiving a card or just thinking about him lifted my spirits. In spite of his hardships, he praised God through it all.

On Easter Sunday, as I was passing through a nearby town, I stopped by Mr. Deal's house to give him a cross and a plaque. I didn't know he was up the street visiting relatives, so I left them in a bag by his back door. He later phoned, telling me about his wonderful day. His relatives had asked how we had become friends. He replied (and I bet with boldness), "It was God!"

In June, during a phone conversation, Mr. Deal admitted that he hadn't yet worn either shirt. "I still show them to people and couldn't have them looking messy," he explained. Before ending our phone call, he concluded, "Maybe I need to hang them up and get them ready to wear." Considering I had sent them nearly eight months earlier, I agreed!

Most often when I phone to ask how he is doing, his praise and thankfulness to God dominate our conversation. "Oh, I'm fine," he would say. "Just my arthritis acting up a little. But I was just so thankful when I got up this morning I could set my feet on the floor and dress myself. God is so good, you know, and I'm so glad He made us friends. I don't really know how all that happened at that sports center, you coming up to me and all, but I'm so thankful that it did."

Acknowledging God's intervention, the two of us remain amazed and humbled at how God—and a medium shirt—connected our lives. God's concern is not about a person's shirt size but about the heart inside the shirt and the acceptance of Jesus in that heart.

Mr. Deal's life is an outpouring of God's love. His faith does not waver; however difficult the battle, he keeps on fighting and believing. He doesn't allow pain and discomfort to steal his joy in life.

"I can do all things through Christ who strengthens me" (Philippians 4:13).

I can do all things through Christ who strengthens me.
Philippians 4:13

Sherman Deal knew the Source of his strength.

This scripture, from the plaque I gave Mr. Deal on Easter, explains Who is in charge of his life. At age eighty-six, the severity of his bent-over body assures me he is walking in God's strength, not his own, while he is experiencing God's love. He knows his cane is only an earthly thing and someday won't be needed.

His strong faith and prayers help him fight his daily battles. Whenever my hand grasps his for a parting prayer, we sense God's blessings on our friendship and give Him the glory for the strength and hope in our lives.

Each time I leave his apartment and head for the elevator, these words echo down the long hallway: "You come back now, ya hear!" Regardless of his pain, he never fails to wait in the hall until the elevator door closes in front of me. As quickly as possible, he resumes his watch from his third-story window that overlooks the parking lot until my car is out of sight.

~~~

On the morning of Mr. Deal's eighty-seventh birthday, I phoned not only to wish him a happy birthday but also to check on his plans for the day. I hoped to stop by for a short visit. He said to come by anytime, that he had no plans. He soon called back to tell me that he would have to pretend not to know his relatives were dropping by for a surprise visit that afternoon. He wasn't sure exactly who or how many, but he wouldn't let me back out, insisting that I come. As I hung up the phone, the thought hit me: *Charge the battery for the camera—a perfect time for pictures.*

I arrived at Mr. Deal's apartment a little before his guests. Excitement filled his eyes. Each time the door opened, a familiar face or two walked in, bringing added joy to his special day. Although familiar to him, they were strangers to me, but not for long. Their warm, caring ways made me feel much like family.

Neatly stacked in front of his television were the Christmas presents I had given him two months earlier, including a new shirt. On top of the pile, I noticed his box of chocolate candy with the cellophane wrapper still intact. He told me that he liked to show his gifts to people and that he was saving his candy for a special occasion like this. When his guests heard that comment, calories went unnoticed!

Shortly after the homemade cake arrived, everyone crowded around the sofa for a group picture. Then, as expected, each family member wanted to pose individually with the birthday celebrity, the person whom they dearly loved and admired. When I would get ready to take a picture, his kinfolk would say, "Smile, Sherman," but his natural expression didn't change. He didn't much appreciate the comments, but he loved his family just the same.

On Mr. Deal's eighty-seventh birthday, his kinfolk crowded around the sofa for a group picture.

With pizza on its way, I insisted that I needed to get on home. After I wished Mr. Deal well, he looked at me with a rather perplexed expression on his face and said, "You're not gonna leave without having our usual prayer, are ya?" We ignored all others as I held his hand in prayer. Before the final *amen*, I asked God's blessings on a most special friend.

As I grabbed my camera on the way to the door, someone handed me an unusually large piece of his birthday cake to take home to eat. I do love cake, especially homemade cake. And I must confess that once I tasted a bit of the frosting, it never made it home.

The following week, Mr. Deal so enjoyed looking at his birthday pictures that he kept his album on his sofa so that everyone could see it. He shared copies of the photos and his story with loved ones

With Jesus in his heart, Mr. Deal continued his journey of life with a cane and a hope.

and friends, not realizing that within months they would be used in celebration of his life.

~~~

On every other Saturday, my husband and I passed by Mr. Deal's apartment on our way through his town. Taking him something to eat became routine. I learned how to load the take-home Styrofoam container from a local restaurant with so much food that Mr. Deal claimed it would last him three meals. At times, he opted for a cheeseburger, fries, and milkshake. On his last Saturday on earth, I called to ask him what he would like on his hamburger that day. He replied, "Everything, and don't forget the onions!"

Four days later, Sherman Deal passed away at home in his third-story apartment with his cane in his hand and hope in his heart. A week or so before his death, a young person on staff had noticed him in the lobby. Like in past months, he was moving from bench to bench, catching his breath on his way to take out his trash. Assuming his back was hurting him, she offered to help. Politely refusing her offer, Mr. Deal replied, "No, ma'am. No, ma'am. I'll be fine. Don't you worry about me, 'cause it won't be long 'til I'll be dancing with Jesus!"

As I began filling my shopping cart with snowmen tree toppers, their carrot-style noses and smiling faces made me want to smile back at them.

CHAPTER TWENTY-TWO

Snowmen, Sheep, and a Savior

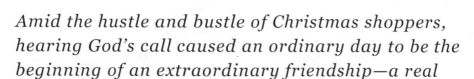

Amid the hustle and bustle of Christmas shoppers, hearing God's call caused an ordinary day to be the beginning of an extraordinary friendship—a real spiritual awakening in life.

With Christmas just around the corner, I made a trip to a nearby town in search of inexpensive gifts. Once inside the store where everything costs a dollar, I looked around a little before I found a shelf neatly lined with snowmen tree toppers. Their attractive knit sweaters and matching hats, along with their carrot-style noses and smiling faces, made me want to smile back at them. I thought to myself, *Those will do just fine*, and began filling my shopping cart.

This caught the attention of a nearby customer. As her eyes examined the contents of my cart, her curiosity got the best of her. With a puzzled look on her face, she questioned, "Why are you buying so many?"

"They're just little gifts for nursing home residents," I replied.

I continued adding snowmen to my cart, while out of the corner of my eye, I noticed her interest in the Santa tree toppers sitting on the same shelf.

"Why don't you buy some of these?" she asked.

Knowing she might possibly buy one herself, I hid my true feelings concerning Santa dominating the real meaning of

Christmas. To answer her question, I suggested that the residents might enjoy the snowmen even after the holidays. And I quickly added, "What matters most is not whether it's a snowman or a Santa, but the 'God Loves You' message attached to each." She seemed satisfied with that answer, and at the end of our brief conversation, she pushed her shopping cart to an adjacent aisle.

Minutes later, while I was removing the last of the snowmen from the shelf, she returned and stopped her cart alongside mine. She had yet another question: "Will the residents have to pay for them?"

"No, they're just little gifts," I answered.

"Oh," she briefly commented and continued on her way.

As she pushed her cart in the opposite direction, my thoughts followed, convincing me of a need I didn't understand. I felt I should send her a true story I had written about a particular person close to my heart.

Without giving it more thought, I approached this stranger in a nearby aisle, told her my name, and explained my intention. She introduced herself as JoAnna, and her kind face and friendly smile made everything seem okay. She said she would like to read my story and allowed me to copy down her address.

She, too, was from out of town, but she resided in an adjacent state. In fact, we discovered that during her forty-five-mile trip that day, she had passed within a half mile of my house. Although our meeting was most unusual, we parted company as newfound friends, unaware of the significant difference that would make in the months ahead.

Days after mailing her the story, I found a mysterious, stuffed manila envelope between several letters in my mailbox. I wondered who had sent it, but not for long. The return address belonged to JoAnna.

As I tore open the gummed flap and pulled out the contents, I couldn't help but smile. Inside was an early and unexpected Christmas gift: a snowman dishtowel with a crocheted top, along with a snowman Christmas card and a lengthy letter. The contents of that package confirmed what I had felt in my heart—she truly was a loving and caring friend.

Although I knew so little about JoAnna, I felt the need to send her a devotional book—like the one I read each day—for her Christmas. I hoped it would be a spiritual blessing to her, unaware of the grief and loneliness that lay ahead.

~~~

In early spring, JoAnna called with devastating news. Her husband had been diagnosed with cancer just days after Christmas, and his four-month battle to fight the disease had recently ended. She wanted me to know how much my story and the daily devotional, *Grace for the Moment*, had helped her cope during those most difficult times. Looking back over the past months, we both knew a loving and all-knowing God had a purpose for connecting our hearts.

Even though she had caring family members living nearby, losing a husband at age sixty-three and not having any children left much loneliness in her life. I sometimes stopped by to see her but seldom found her at home.

Because she was solely responsible for paying the bills, she withstood a tremendous workload. Her weekly schedule involved a lengthy morning drive before sunup to a job at a furniture factory. In midafternoon, she traveled to the family farm to do her share of the chores—a responsibility that didn't end on Saturdays and Sundays.

Her stamina and perseverance after the death of her husband seemed quite remarkable. I remember asking how she managed to cope so well. I can still hear her say, "I put one foot in front of the other and keep on going. You gotta do what you gotta do." She and I both knew Who was giving her that strength.

~~~

A few months later, I found myself the only customer in a store, looking for a friendship card to send JoAnna. Meanwhile, another person entered the store and began talking with employees. From where I was standing, I couldn't see her face, but something about the voice seemed incredibly familiar. I thought, *It couldn't be, could it?*

I left the card section and spotted this customer shopping in another aisle. Because her back was toward me, I took a chance and softly called out, "JoAnna?" Her head turned quickly in surprise, leaving me no less amazed. Hearing her speak my name removed all doubt.

Just like old friends, we stretched out our arms and greeted one another with a warm hug. Both of us laughed and admitting we didn't remember exactly what the other one looked like from our short visit the previous year. Oddly enough, our paths crossed the second time while we were shopping in the same chain of stores in a different town.

~~~

The following March was a particularly busy month, especially with Easter arriving unusually early. On the Saturday before Easter, a stack of cards intended for residents at a nursing home in a nearby town remained on my kitchen table. I felt disappointed for not getting them mailed, but I didn't have the energy to deliver them.

About five o'clock that afternoon, I heard an unexpected knock on the sliding glass door. There stood JoAnna holding a beautifully wrapped hyacinth. This second visit was quite a surprise, for we lived fifteen miles apart, and she had already delivered an Easter card and cookies weeks earlier. She explained that when she saw that blooming flower, she felt she was supposed to bring it to me.

I thanked her and invited her to take a look at my refrigerator door in hopes she'd recognize the Easter card. She pointed to the little lamb on the front and claimed it looked exactly like those she cared for on the family farm. "You've got to come see them sometime," she commented.

It was very late in the afternoon, and she mentioned needing to get on her way. She had one more stop to make. It was at a nursing home—the same nursing home where my cards needed to be delivered!

The following week, each time I passed by the refrigerator door, I remembered JoAnna's invitation. I love photography and longed to take pictures of her little lambs, especially after I had heard about the set of twins. That being my son's profession, I found him most willing to make a trip home and accompany me on my upcoming visit to her farm.

When JoAnna answered her cell phone that Saturday morning, I could detect by the sound of her voice that something was wrong. She was standing in the parking lot of a car dealership, trying to find a replacement for her worn-out car. Making that decision was stress enough but not the root of the problem. Her heart was grieving, for that day marked the one-year anniversary of her

JoAnna claimed that the little lamb on the front of this card looked just like the ones she cared for on the family farm.

husband's passing. But regardless of her circumstances, she didn't allow her feelings to spoil our plans for the following day.

Because the roads to the farm were off the beaten path and unfamiliar to John and me, JoAnna thought it best we meet in a designated location after church. She rode with her brother in the lead vehicle to make sure we didn't get lost. With cameras charged and ready, we anxiously followed.

After we traveled a five-mile stretch of highway and side roads, my son and I got our first glimpse of the sheep grazing on a distant hillside. As we traveled on, those wooly animals became a familiar sight on each side of the road. We parked our vehicle and grabbed our camera gear, anticipating some once-in-a-lifetime shots.

The sheep in their natural environment reminded me of biblical times—rocky pastureland and hilly terrain, streams of trickling water, and worn dirt paths where many hoofs had traveled. Throughout the warm afternoon hours, the frequent clicks of our cameras disrupted the natural quiet of the day.

Later that afternoon, to help us get the best possible shots, JoAnna called out loudly to the sheep that were grazing in a nearby pasture. They recognized and responded to her voice. As incredible as it seemed, the young to the old stopped what they were doing and fell in line to follow her. Once inside the protection of the pen, they were given a little silage to nibble on. One little lamb snuggled close to its wooly mother. I never imagined such joy from photographing sheep in a place so close to home.

Several breeds of donkeys grazed in the hillside pastures alongside the sheep. JoAnna told us that the donkeys protected the sheep from wild dogs. Sometimes, when the donkeys thought we had become a little too close, they positioned themselves between the sheep and our lenses, reminding us of their territorial rights.

Recognizing JoAnna's voice, countless sheep of all sizes stopped nibbling on grass and followed her across the open pasture to this nearby pen.

One little lamb snuggled close to its wooly mother.

A humbling thought to consider: *God created this Egyptian breed of donkey and branded it with a cross for Jesus to ride to His birth and through the streets of Jerusalem the week of His death.*

Learning about and photographing the Sicilian donkeys became the highlight of the afternoon. JoAnna pointed out that each of these donkeys had been born with a dark, cross-shaped marking the entire length and width of their back. In fact, it looked as if someone had branded a cross on them. She told us of their Egyptian origin and how this particular breed has become widely accepted as the one Mary and Joseph rode into Bethlehem and Jesus rode through the streets of Jerusalem on Palm Sunday. Jesus' entrance into Jerusalem on a colt, the foal of a donkey, is prophesized in the Old Testament in the book of Zechariah and is documented in the New Testament by all four gospel writers.

I believe the cross marking is visible proof that God is all-knowing, that He knew at the time of creation of the cross His Son would bear. It is humbling to think God created this breed with a sweet, affectionate disposition and branded it with a cross for Jesus to ride to His birth and through the streets of Jerusalem the week of His death. My son and I left JoAnna's farm that day with something more important than the pictures on our cameras—new truths in our hearts.

~~~

Months later, JoAnna called with exciting news—a baby Sicilian donkey had been born. I thought, *What a sight to behold!* My son and I soon made another trip with our cameras to her farm.

Before we could photograph this colt, JoAnna laughingly admitted, "We'll first have to find him!" The two of us climbed into the front seat of the Gator, but her long-haired sheepdog, Angel, had no intention of being left behind. Before we had time to react, she jumped aboard and squeezed in between the two of us. With

Not wanting to be left behind, JoAnna's sheepdog, Angel, jumped aboard the Gator and squeezed in between us.

no other seat available, John squatted down behind us and held onto a safety bar to steady himself and protect his camera gear. As we took off across rough terrain on a bumpy ride in search of that baby colt, a sudden breeze cooled our faces, and laughter filled the air.

All at once the noisy Gator slowed and then came to an abrupt stop. As we looked in the distance across a grassy field, we spotted a group of donkeys: the mother, the father, and the baby Sicilian colt, among others. Although its legs still a bit wobbly, the recently born colt proudly stood tall. Our cameras were equipped with special lenses, but trying to casually move in close enough without attracting attention called for more than perseverance—it called for bribery!

Although the designated feeding time was late afternoon and JoAnna wanted to stay on schedule, she coaxed one of the donkeys into being more friendly and cooperative by offering it a sampling of its upcoming meal. When the donkey lowered its head to eat, the cross marking became more visible. Finding the best angle to fully show this marking became most challenging to the point of my son climbing atop a storage building. Many clicks followed. We checked our camera screens, believing such pictures were worth a thousand words.

JoAnna truly loved these animals, and their affection for her was obvious. As I walked back across the pastureland in her direction, she stood hugging two of the older donkeys that had lingered up from adjacent fields.

While she was stroking their necks, JoAnna explained some of their backgrounds, which involved three generations. The father of the colt had been purchased when extremely thin. In fact, the scars from slash marks could be seen across his body and legs, evidence

Although its legs still a bit wobbly, the recently born colt—a baby Sicilian donkey—proudly stood tall.

Spending time with JoAnna and her farm animals was a gift from God, just like our friendship.

of being whipped and abused. When she spoke those words, I was reminded of a similar occurrence told by all four gospel writers.

No less amazing was the history behind some of the donkeys' names. Although the colt had not yet been named, its mother's name was Easter because of her birth on Easter. Another female was named Palm, having been born on Palm Sunday. Needless to say, I considered spending time with JoAnna and her farm animals a gift from God, just like our friendship.

~~~

The Bible refers to Jesus as the Lamb of God. The need for sacrificing unblemished lambs as recorded in the Old Testament ended with Jesus' sacrificial death on the cross in the New Testament. Living a sinless life, Jesus paid the ultimate price once and for all because of His great love for us.

Scripture compares Jesus to a shepherd, and we, to His sheep. Sheep have the ability to hear their master's voice. But without someone to lead them, they are lost. The same is true for us.

"My sheep hear my voice, and I know them, and they follow Me. I give them eternal life, and they shall never perish; neither shall anyone snatch them out of My hand" (John 10:27-28 NKJV).

In his book, *Safe in the Shepherd's Arms*, Max Lucado expresses it this way: "If you have the Shepherd, you have grace for every sin, direction for every turn, a candle for every corner, and an anchor for every storm. You have everything you need."

Throughout our recent years of friendship, JoAnna and I have heard the Shepherd's voice and continue to give Him the glory. We know God purposefully connected our lives through snowmen, sheep, and most importantly, our Savior.

CHAPTER TWENTY-THREE

More than a Dream

God works in mysterious ways. Once He revealed His will through a dream and a corduroy cap.

Members of a small community church expressed differing views concerning the possible purchase of an old elementary school. Since the school's closing, severe vandalism had decreased its value, which left the school board no option but to sell or demolish. They decided to offer its sale by sealed bids.

The church members stood firm in their individual convictions regarding its purchase. Uncle Perk, along with others who voiced opposition, thought it unwise to take on an additional financial burden. Members in favor of the purchase tried to convince them to change their minds.

Regardless of prior discussions, on the Sunday before the bidding, consensus failed. The inability to reach an agreement caused much concern. At the close of the worship service, families left for their respective homes with the issue unresolved.

After a filling lunch at home, Uncle Perk headed for his favorite Sunday afternoon spot—the couch. But the peaceful, anticipated rest didn't happen. He awoke abruptly from a dream, emotionally shaken and in tears. In his dream, Uncle Perk was told that he was to buy the property for the church and was given the exact figure to bid.

Feeling responsible, he immediately called a meeting of the

church deacons. When all had arrived, he displayed unexpected tears as he emotionally shared what the Lord had revealed to him through a dream. He then proposed to donate the money for the old school building with one restriction: The building was to be bought in the church's name but not named after the church, with hope of benefiting the entire community. The deacons agreed to his request. Uncle Perk felt confident in the amount to bid. Yet everyone knew that if the bid was too low and rejected, the opportunity would be gone.

The school board opened bids the following Monday as planned. The church's offer perfectly matched the lowest acceptable bid. Word of Uncle Perk's dream circulated in the community. A dream and a step of faith helped to end the threat of demolition. When ownership changed hands, the old school building became officially named *Family Life Center*.

According to one church member, "Buying this facility seemed to unite the church in closer fellowship. It took a lot of effort on the part of its members to make this outdated school usable. Even during the time of renovation, vandalism continued, adding expense and disappointment to those involved. Much glass had been broken. Kids had even been caught skateboarding on the building's flat roof!"

As our conversation continued, he told how the benefits outweighed the drawbacks. The front section of the building accommodated large social gatherings for anyone in the community. I remember when Uncle Perk threw an eightieth birthday party for our aunt there. Another section was filled with pews and set apart for worship. This proved especially beneficial for members of a neighboring church after a fire damaged their facility. Also, as the bus ministry increased, more community children participated in a

Uncle Perk threw an eightieth birthday party for his wife in the building he had purchased for community use after acting on a dream.

spiritual growth program, which included snacks and recreational activities in the gym. The purchase of the unused school allowed the church's mission statement, "To share God's love and message of salvation with others," to become a greater reality.

Uncle Perk's unexpected death caused by a farming accident left a void in the hearts of many. Those who knew him remembered his love and commitment to God, his church, his family, his neighbors, and his friends. Because of his strong faith and fun-loving nature, his presence continues to be sadly missed. His life made a great impact on the lives of many, especially mine, and even on the life of a stranger.

~~~

Months after his untimely death, his favorite cap remained hanging on a hook inside the back door where he had left it. The fond remembrance of Uncle Perk wearing that tan corduroy cap on cool days complicated the decision to give it away. God knew my heart ached when I had to acknowledge that the cap needed a new owner, and I counted on His help in finding that special person.

Weeks later, not knowing what else to do, I placed the cap in a sack and headed for a personal care facility that housed predominately male residents. As I stepped inside the lobby, one particular man came to mind. His name was Gerald.

I walked down the hallway in search of this man and found him sitting in his room on the side of his bed. I noticed the neat and tidy contents of his room and remembered his kind and polite ways. Offering him the contents of the sack seemed like the right thing to do.

He graciously accepted the corduroy cap. He noticed its fine quality and considered it a step above the ordinary, everyday cap. But he seemed most amazed at the story behind the cap. He listened attentively as I told about my uncle's dream and his strong faith in Jesus.

Knowing the owner of that cap has continued to be a blessing to me. Gerald meticulously cares for the cap as a treasure and keeps it displayed on top of his dresser. I smile when I see him wearing it on chilly days, whether he's enjoying a bit of fresh air around the facility, taking a leisurely walk up a nearby road, or entering a local church.

Recently, Gerald shared his faith experience with me: "It was around 1968. I was on my deathbed in the hospital with rheumatic fever, and I accepted Jesus. The pastor of the church came over and had prayer. I joined the church after I got back home and accepted Jesus as my Savior—both my wife and me. I was baptized, dunked under. I started taking the kids to church. I took part in it; I passed the hat around," he said with a sort of a chuckle. "You know, they have a collection plate to take up money for the church. That was done every Sunday." Then he made a slight correction and said, "They passed the Lord's Supper around and then the collection plate."

Gerald made several comments regarding his deathbed and the close timing of his commitment. I said in response, "Gerald, as long as there is breath in you, it is never too late."

"That's right. That's right," he agreed.

But unspoken thoughts lingered in our minds: *No one knows for certain when that last breath will be.*

~~~

Days later, I stopped by the personal care facility to take Gerald extra copies of his story. He wanted to share these with relatives, along with his photo—the picture of him wearing Uncle Perk's cap. Becoming friends and writing a story because of a cap seemed rather incredible to both Gerald and me.

As I was walking out the door to leave, I said, "Gerald, someday when you get to heaven, I believe you will meet Uncle Perk."

With a look of contentment on his face, he added, "And we'll have something to talk about."

Gerald's acceptance of Uncle Perk's cap was important to me, but nothing compared to his acceptance of Jesus in his heart. When I see my friend proudly wearing this cap, I am reminded of Uncle Perk. I remember his humor, his compassion, his faith, and his dream, which was much more than a dream. I believe it was God's will, like the sharing of the cap.

My son, John, loved helping his "Aunt Betty" give the flowers a drink.

CHAPTER TWENTY-FOUR

Beyond a Mother's Grief

Unexpected grief plagued the heart of a mother, but her unwavering faith and the outpouring of her love helped heal her pain and prepare her heart for the challenging days ahead.

I became acquainted with Betty because of my love for flowers and plants, considering them God's little miracles. She and her husband, Jim, owned a nearby nursery, and I longed to rent a little space in one of their greenhouses to test my green thumb. Instead, they offered me a job to help care for two greenhouses and a covered shadehouse full of plants.

Betty and Jim became not only my employers and close friends but also my first babysitters. Because they were such special people in my young son's life, he called them "Aunt Betty" and "Uncle Jim."

When my son, John, reached the age of two, he acted as if he were on their payroll. He loved *helping* his Aunt Betty. He assumed such responsibilities as carrying the red geraniums to new locations, cutting the grass with his plastic mower, and turning on the hose to give the flowers a drink—or anyone in sight! And pretending to drive Uncle Jim's tractor was especially fun when Aunt Betty hopped on for a ride. Those were a few of the precious memories we made before moving miles away.

Pretending to drive Uncle Jim's tractor was especially fun
when Aunt Betty hopped on for a ride.

~~~

Heartbreaking days followed. Within months, their adult son was on trial for a most serious offense. A phone call prompted me to support the family on the final day of his sentencing. How I dreaded each mile of the two-hour trip! Reaching my destination meant facing reality and acknowledging the devastation in the lives of people whom I dearly loved.

As soon as I spotted Betty and Jim outside the courtroom, we hugged one another. They seemed certain I would be there. The stressed look on their faces told of the despair and heartache that had plagued them for months. Jim asked that I sit with the family during the trial, but because I felt too overwhelmed by it all, I just couldn't.

Everyone walked through metal detectors before they entered the courtroom. Security was quite intense. Uniformed officers stood alert at all exits and encircled the balcony overlooking the courtroom. Television cameras provided live coverage for a local station, allowing it to become a daily soap opera. I sat alone throughout the trial, hurting inside for everyone involved, wondering what the verdict would be.

The judge's pronouncement of the sentence "life imprisonment" seemed almost unbearable, but it could have been worse—the death sentence by electric chair. When law officials handcuffed the son and led him out of the courtroom to begin serving his life sentence, I could hardly watch. After the trial, I shared a few words with Betty and Jim, but I mostly gave hugs. Faith helped sustain all of us through those most difficult days.

Later, I exchanged letters with their son. If he were to share a message from his prison cell, he would urge others to stay off drugs—all drugs. He would say, "Don't ever start!" He admitted that after using drugs frequently, he no longer was in control of them; they controlled him. The high from drugs gave him only a temporary burst of freedom. Their use resulted in the removal of his freedom. Barbed-wire fences, armed guards, and prison cells bar him from society. His life is proof that the effect of being obsessed with watching heinous movies and being addicted to cocaine should never be underestimated.

For more than twenty years, Betty and Jim have continued to faithfully travel to the prison and meet with their son at their appointed time each week. Although two hours may not seem like much of a visit, it provides the only substitute for special family times that are no longer possible.

~~~

Instead of allowing that tragic event to steal her passion in life, Betty turned heartfelt grief into action. After she heard about Aunt Mary's Storybook Project, a prison ministry to help unite children with parents, she knew this was her calling. This program arranges for incarcerated parents to read books to their children on audiocassettes and for the book and tape to be mailed to the intended child as a gift.

With the help of her church family, Betty initiated the program at a women's correctional facility close to where her son was serving his sentence. Thankful her son had earned his associate degree while in prison, she commented, "Helping with the project at the women's facility was my way of giving back to the prison system on behalf of my son."

After she had been involved in this outreach for over ten years, Betty arranged for my security clearance so I could join the volunteer ladies from her church and observe the ministry firsthand. The morning of their scheduled visit, the weather became miserably hot and humid—the worst that July.

As the church van pulled into the parking lot, the silver metal on the highly coiled, barbed-wire fences that surrounded the facility reflected the sun's bright rays, drawing attention to the facility's security. Inside this restricted area, nearly a thousand women resided, separated from society and their families and, most sadly, their children.

Passing through the armed security check and securing our badges at registration presented no problem. Then Betty, with the help of a cane and my hand, began the long walk through cooled hallways to the heat-reflecting sidewalks outside the main facility. In the distance, we spotted our destination—a beautiful stone chapel with stained-glass windows, the site of the outreach project for young mothers.

Female inmates who participated in this program arrived according to a designated schedule. After they signed in, they searched through plastic crates containing a large selection of age-appropriate books—new and beautifully illustrated—to find a special book for each of their children. As soon as a side room became available, a mother accompanied a sponsor into the privacy of that room to read aloud each story while a tape player recorded her voice. At the end of the session, volunteers placed each tape and book in an envelope to be mailed to the child.

Betty invited me to sit with her behind closed doors. Although a bit nervous and emotional, the first young mother soon relaxed as she began telling us about her four children, the youngest being eighteen months. She then opened one of her selected books and began reading into a recorder.

At the conclusion of each book, wanting to be strong and convincing, the mother tried her best to blink back the tears as she spoke into the recorder, "Mommy loves you, and I'll be home soon." Hearing those words was enough to break anyone's heart. I could only imagine each child's response at the sound of the mother's voice. I sat in on several of those sessions and watched young mothers try to sooth the pain caused by separation and lack of hugs.

Betty's grief caused her to lovingly reach out to others with the same need—the need for parents to be reunited with their children. Separation is painful, regardless of age, as Betty well knows. But because of health problems, participating in that outreach became increasingly difficult. A flare-up of back problems resulted in three major surgeries, which brought little or no improvement in her condition. Regardless, Betty's perseverance kept her active in this worthwhile prison ministry.

For years, on a Friday evening during the month of December, Betty and other members of her church's handbell choir traveled to the prison where her son was incarcerated. Prior to the performance in the chapel, he posted signs encouraging others to attend. Refreshments followed. With her son in attendance, this became a highlight of the Christmas season.

Another prison-related outreach for Betty and Jim involved welcoming a stranger into the privacy of their home. At the son's request, they responded to the needs of an ex-cellmate who had no place to go after he was released. For years, they set aside a portion of their basement as his living quarters and often set a place for him at their kitchen table, helping him adjust to his new role in society.

Although both Betty and her husband faced significant health issues, they were determined to go on a much deserved dream vacation, an Alaskan cruise. The bank where my husband worked sponsored a similar trip. Not until their return did I learn that the travel agency paired those two groups—located some hundred fifty miles apart—to travel together.

Some of the local people who had gone on the cruise smiled at the mention of Betty and Jim. They considered them friends, admiring them for their determination to make such a trip. They told of Jim pushing Betty in a wheelchair in spite of his own health problems and of their love and devotion to one another. This couple's cheerful smiles, upbeat attitudes, and perseverance impressed even strangers who knew nothing about the sadness that lingered in their hearts.

~~~

When I phoned Betty prior to Christmas, she had just returned from another physical therapy session, aware that something continued to adversely affect her muscles and speech. Regardless of her health, she pushed on and coped the best she could each day. She explained the reason for missing my call earlier in the week: "I was a bell ringer for the Salvation Army for our church. Because it's hard finding volunteers, Jim and I do a lot of it." They were also busy wrapping poinsettias for their church, a job they had assumed for more than twenty years.

As she began telling about a prison outreach program, I could sense the commitment in her heart. She and Jim would be delivering hundreds of donated candy bars, children's books, both mittens and gloves, and Christmas stockings to a collection center at her son's prison the following day. This statewide drive furnishes Christmas stockings for some seven thousand children who would be visiting the prisons during the Christmas season. Once again, Betty's heartfelt response makes a difference.

Before she hung up the phone, she had one more thing to tell me. In spite of her health, she and Jim would soon be traveling to the tropical islands of Hawaii. For a couple that had spent most of their lifetime caring for flowers and plants and also for others, this seemed to be the ultimate trip. On the postcard later sent to me, Betty simply described it, "Beautiful." Remembering our past, she humorously added at the end of her note, "You and I could get a job over there watering flowers!"

~~~

The welcome mat outside Betty and Jim's back door literally means what it says. Their acceptance of others allowed me to invite my elderly friend, Genie, to their home to celebrate his birthday. The drive to Genie's house took hours, but the trip from Genie's place to Betty's took only minutes.

Because of past "coincidences" in their lives, their meeting was a long-awaited moment. Betty had sold me the mum that I had taken to Genie's mom, a stranger, the day before she died—the same day I met Genie. And now, some twenty-seven years later, Betty and Genie, who have known one another only through me, have finally met on his eighty-second birthday.

Prior to our little party, Genie and I stopped at a fast food restaurant for a hamburger. As we made conversation, I asked if he remembered any particular birthdays. "No, not really," was his response.

He then elaborated a bit. He told me that when he was growing up and throughout his life, money just wasn't there. He said they never had any gifts or cakes or anything like that. He described his birthdays as "typical, just like every other day—another ho-hum day like Christmas." So hard to imagine! *Never a cake?*

Because Genie had no working television, part of the planned celebration was watching a Daniel O'Donnell concert on DVD at Betty's house. How Genie's life had previously connected with Mr. O'Donnell, an Irish entertainer, is another story, but I will mention this: Recently, when Mr. O'Donnell greeted guests after the taping of his Nashville concert, he said to me, "How's Genie? I want you to tell Genie hello from me."

Knowing only a handful of people, Genie had found it simply amazing that someone from across the ocean would ever notice him. Others thought the same, including me. Watching his concert on DVD took on new meaning for all of us. I left the DVD for Betty and Jim, along with his *Peace in the Valley* album, knowing the blessing this music would bring to their lives.

The increased darkness by the setting sun told us it was time to get on with the party. We gathered around the kitchen table with the decorated cake sitting in front of Genie. After the three of us sang "Happy Birthday," he blew out the candles. We then paused, thanking God for connecting our lives and for our many blessings.

After Genie finished eating his second piece of cake, he picked up the package sitting beside him that had been tied with curling ribbon. With a puzzled look on his face, he asked, "Now just how am I supposed to open this?"

Watching a Daniel O'Donnell concert at the "mum" lady's house, Genie had found it simply amazing that someone from across the ocean would ever notice him.

Never having had gifts or cake for his birthday, Genie gazed at his first cake as the three of us sang "Happy Birthday."

On his way out the door, Genie shook hands with Betty, "the mum lady," thankful for her hospitality on his birthday and for the special ways God had connected their lives.

Jim suggested Genie get out his pocketknife, remarking that he, "being an old-timer," would probably be carrying one. When Genie slipped one out of his pocket, Jim, an antique dealer, recognized the knife and casually remarked that it would probably bring forty dollars or so.

I couldn't help but tease Jim a bit by saying, "I now understand why you offered Genie a seat in your big recliner. You were probably hoping Genie's knife would fall out of his pocket so you could keep it and resell it!" Considering how far from the truth that statement was, we all had a laugh.

With his knife, Genie cut each ribbon tied around his gifts. He received enough CDs to entertain him for days, maybe even weeks, including a gift set of the Stanley Brothers from the 1960s and Daniel O'Donnell's life story on audio along with a music CD. He backed his chair away from the table before he stood up to try on his new vest. We all agreed. It fit.

Late that afternoon as Genie and I headed for the door, he stopped to shake hands with "the mum lady", thankful for her hospitality on his birthday and for the special ways God had connected their lives. But if Genie couldn't understand her speech because of health issues, he certainly knew her heart. Genie didn't make any fuss about taking home the leftover cake.

After I gave Jim and Betty a hug and thanked them for being a part of this celebration, I wished them well and a safe trip— their daughter was accompanying them on an upcoming cruise to the Caribbean Islands. With Betty's health issues advancing, how could they take another cruise? Perseverance and God's grace were the answers.

~~~

Everyone who knows Betty Collier will agree, her perseverance is incredible, in spite of grief and unexpected
health issues. Betty truly has a servant's heart.

Sometimes hearts are connected in a special way, but not until looking back in these later years did I realize the true significance of knowing Betty. Sharing not only our joy and happiness in life but also our tears of sadness made this friendship priceless. Even though we have lived miles apart for many years, we keep in touch as special memories remain in our hearts. I consider Betty one of those rare forever friends.

Betty has refused to allow life's tough circumstances to steal her joy and passion. In spite of her grief and unexpected health issues, her perseverance is incredible. Her purposeful and Christ-centered life is an outpouring of God's love. Everyone who knows Betty Collier will agree—she truly has a servant's heart.

CHAPTER TWENTY-FIVE

A Purse, a Prayer and an Irish Blessing

Waiting in line often tests my patience. I never found that experience incredibly amazing or worth remembering, until—

Trying to find special flowers for my aunt's ninety-second birthday, I stopped at the floral department of a large grocery store. By arriving early in the day, I avoided the normal rush of Saturday morning shoppers. But considering the flowers quite expensive, I decided to look elsewhere.

With only a birthday card to buy, I walked past the nearest checkout lanes with no waiting and chose the one farthest away. I noticed an elderly lady there, sitting in the store's motorized shopping cart, patiently waiting her turn. I sensed her loneliness and stood quietly in line behind her, but not for long.

With a friendly smile on her face, she glanced over her shoulder and invited me to go in front of her. Even though she had only a few items, she explained that writing a check would take her extra time. At first I declined, thinking that would be rude. But because of her insistence and the thought of my husband waiting in the car, I accepted the offer and thanked her for being so kind. Her adept driving skills impressed me as she maneuvered the motorized cart in reverse. After we switched places in line, I turned to visit with her.

I mentioned my aunt's birthday and commented on the store's beautiful but expensive roses. The lady listened attentively and agreed that the flowers were overpriced. She then told about when her daughter had bought her roses. With a bit of humor, she added, "I was glad to get them while I was living and could enjoy them!" Still thinking of her daughter, she proudly remarked, "She's a schoolteacher."

I thought to myself, *That sounds a lot like me.* I explained how I enjoyed giving my mother roses while she was living, and that I, too, was a schoolteacher. Immediately, the song "Give Me the Roses While I Live" came to mind. I told her about an elderly man recording that song for me, and that I had written a story about him.

"Oh, you write stories? I write poems. In fact, if you wait just a moment—"

With her head tilted down and a determined look on her face, she began searching and rearranging items in the purse that rested on her lap. Before long, she handed me a copy of the poem, "Looking Back," that she had written one New Year's Day while a patient in a hospital.

The poem that beautifully portrayed her thoughts allowed me to put a name with her face, and from then on, I knew her as Donnabelle. As I acknowledged her for her giftedness and thanked her for the poem, her hand again disappeared into her purse.

This time, she removed a white envelope of favorite photos. Her face beamed with happiness as she shared the picture of her daughter's family, naming and telling a little about each person, especially the four grandchildren. But suddenly, when she handed me a snapshot of a cute little black and white dog, the expression on her face saddened and the tone of her voice drastically changed.

Looking Back

Looking back over the year that is past,
Think only of the joys that will truly last.
Think not of the unkind word
Or anything "negative" that you have heard.
There will always be the good and the bad,
The happy times, the lonely, and the sad;
Life is a mixture of all these,
And the "trying" times won't always please.
But after the clouds, and the rain pours down,
The clouds disappear and so does the frown.
A smile can be seen, 'twill gladden the heart,
And we have a chance to make a new start.
For to each of us God gives a brand new day;
We can be happy as we go on our way,
Or we can complain of our lot in life
And harbor in our hearts both bitterness and strife.
But we are the ones who suffer and grieve
If we don't have forgiveness for those who deceive.
So, let us start out in the grand year ahead,
Not remembering the bad but the good times instead,
Rejoicing each new day and each precious minute
For all of God's blessings that He has placed in it.

—*Donnabelle Adams*

"I'm so lonesome," she admitted. "My little dog died, and I miss her so much." I could hardly believe her words; I had recently experienced the same heartache. A most unusual conversation ended as I paid the cashier.

When I reached the door, the thought of never seeing her again bothered me. I felt the need to stay in touch. Despite my attempt to get back to my waiting husband, I returned to the checkout lane.

As soon as Donnabelle moved the motorized cart out of the path of shoppers, I spoke with her again. I offered to mail her the story about my guitar-playing friend. Without hesitating, her hand slipped once again into her purse and then reappeared with an address label that already had her phone number written across the top. I couldn't help but smile, thinking how incredibly prepared this lady was: the poem, the pictures, and the address labels—all accessible in her purse. We left the store friends, regardless of the twenty miles that separated our homes.

~~~

A few days after mailing Donnabelle the story, I received a beautifully penned, eight-page letter and a copy of *Poems and Meditations*, her published booklet from the 1970s. After reading several selections, I recognized the servant's heart of my gifted friend.

In past years, as is told in her booklet, Donnabelle found inspiration for writing while at church and during revivals, but more often, while under a hair dryer or in her kitchen. She noted that one lengthy poem even caused her cookies to burn! One sleepless night, she wrote a poem by flashlight at the kitchen counter at 4:40 a.m. Another night, when illness kept her awake, she composed the poem, "Why Have I Become Ill?"

Donnabelle's published booklet from the 1970s exposed the servant's heart of my gifted friend.

Why Have I Become Ill?

Lord, I have striven to do Thy will.
I can't understand why I've become ill.
Perhaps You knew I needed the rest,
Because You always give the best.

My duties so many are left undone.
And there are souls that need to be won.
I want to gain strength to start anew.
My life must be pleasing, always to You.

If through my illness more souls I can win,
Help me be patient and peaceful within.
If it's only to reach someone through a letter,
I can do this till you help me get better.

2:20 a.m., home—can't sleep

—Donnabelle Adams

On my first trip to visit Donnabelle, she greeted me with a hug and graciously invited me inside. Her love of music dominated the modest room that served as both living quarters and bedroom. Inspirational songs sung by Daniel O'Donnell softly filled the air. A keyboard sat beside her small television. Donnabelle shared photos of her and her sisters as young musicians playing guitar and singing gospel music. She dearly loved reminiscing about those days of youth, telling of her father's ministry and family travels to nearby states to witness for the Lord.

My friend continued her life's story by sharing remembrances of the Great Depression and the years of prosperity that followed. She explained how serious health issues had led to life-threatening surgeries. She relived a terrible day in the 1980s when a fire had burned her home and destroyed almost everything. What little she had salvaged fit in her car as she moved to the town where she presently lives.

At the end of my first visit, Donnabelle shared feelings of loneliness. "A lot of my friends have passed away. No one comes to see me like they used to. I prayed to God for a friend, and you were an answer to prayer."

In spite of her circumstances, Donnabelle doesn't allow her lack of possessions and physical hardship to diminish her faith in God. She claims, "God has been good to me. He had a reason for sparing my life after major surgeries. Many people prayed for me." Her most recent back surgery brought relief but not freedom from pain. A cane and a walker help her to get around, but she acknowledges her greatest help comes from God.

~~~

Since the day we first met at the grocery, flowers continue to be a topic of conversation. One morning, Donnabelle phoned to tell me about a zinnia coming up voluntarily in her backyard. Over time, it produced numerous blooms and grew incredibly tall. With a yardstick in one hand and her cane in the other, she kept track of its growth and kept me informed. On one particular visit, we counted over thirty blooms as it literally towered above her head. Rather astonished by its growth, she remarked, "To think it just came up. Wasn't the Lord good to us to send us that pretty flower?" We both had a history of growing zinnias, but this plant was most unusual.

Months later, a ravaging storm that had started as a hurricane in the Gulf traveled hundreds of miles before it hit our area. Devastating winds blew for hours like nothing we had ever witnessed. Although little structural damage occurred, uprooted trees and broken limbs showed evidence of its destructive nature. When phone service was restored, my friend expressed more disappointment in the bent-over condition of one zinnia plant than in the huge tree limbs that blocked her front walk!

~~~

I seldom hear Donnabelle complain unless there is a problem with her car. She claims the driver's seat of her '88 Oldsmobile is more comfortable than any seat she owns. Over this past year, besides the daily in-town trips, her worn-out vehicle traveled many hundreds of miles to visit family members. She loves being out and about, but having the strength to endure long trips and the means to keep the car up and running can be a challenge. When

Despite the stiffness of her fingers and her back pain, Donnabelle continues to use her God-given talent to witness for the Lord.

mechanics claimed her vehicle wasn't worth fixing, her prayers were answered by an understanding church family. At times such as these, she often quotes a favorite scripture: "And we know that in all things God works for the good of those who love him, who have been called according to his purpose" (Romans 8:28).

My friend is seldom at a loss for words, whether written or spoken. She recalls names, dates, and details from the distant past like no one I have ever met. During our friendship, she has sent me well over fifty pieces of mail, seldom leaving a square inch of blank space. In addition to writing lengthy letters, she loves receiving them, for she considers mail the highlight of her day.

If it's not time for the postman and she's feeling lonely, she often drives to a nearby store to find someone to talk with, claiming she never meets a stranger, or at least not for long. Another favorite spot is anywhere she can find a complimentary copy of her local newspaper to read, especially at a fast food restaurant, even though she often denies herself the privilege of buying something to eat.

~~~

Regardless of the hardships and trials, Donnabelle lives a humble life at age eighty-six, serving and glorifying God. Despite the stiffness of her fingers and the back pain that lingers, she continues to use her God-given talent to witness for the Lord.

Donnabelle was born to sing; it is her life. She is a member of the senior choir of a large church located close to her home. When able, she packs up her walker and heads to a local nursing home in the hopes to find a vacant seat on the piano bench, to visit the lonely, or to sing with her church choir. I've heard her sweet singing in public, but more often, while playing her keyboard at home. Occasionally, she sings over the phone. But I most remember the time I took her to have a tooth pulled.

After surgery, she sat in my car, tapping her finger up and down along the lower side of her jaw and even on her nose, informing me how numb it was. Trying to keep her spirits up, I remembered her past and jokingly said, "Be glad you don't have to sing at a wedding!" My words awakened her memory, and she started singing. The dentist would certainly not have recommended the laughter that followed!

~~~

No matter where I go, Donnabelle remains in my heart, and Branson, Missouri, is no exception. For the past couple of years, my husband and I vacationed there in late fall.

During the morning of our first visit, instead of leaving the dining room of our motel with my husband, I felt I had to return to a table where a couple of strangers were seated. I'm not certain what attracted me to them, but possibly it was their kind, friendly faces or the gentleman's fine Texan hat. I asked if they had seen any particularly good shows. When the wife responded, "Daniel O'Donnell," I couldn't help but smile. The possibility of seeing him in person seemed too good to be true.

Without the friendship of Donnabelle, his name would have meant nothing to me, for she had been the one who had introduced me to his singing. Because of her, I constantly played his CDs and watched his past performances that aired on public television, finding his music most uplifting. I knew his homeland was Ireland and that he sometimes appeared in the States, but I had been unaware of his Branson connection. Thankfully, our vacation fell during the three weeks of his appearances.

Acting on the advice of the friendly couple, my husband and I wasted no time getting to the ticket office. Of the theater's two thousand plus seats, only four tickets remained unsold. We felt incredibly blessed to be a part of the audience. Mr. O'Donnell's show was not only entertaining, but through the words of his songs, he shared a message of hope and inspiration.

During intermission, I stepped outside the theater to use my cell phone to call Donnabelle. I could hardly wait to tell her the news about her favorite singer performing in Branson. She, too, was surprised. Before I returned to my seat, I remembered Donnabelle's love of reading and bought her a book about Mr. O'Donnell's mother. After the show, being incredibly accessible to his fans, he kindly signed it: "Donnabelle, love, Daniel," making that day the highlight of our trip.

~~~

This past fall before packing my suitcase for Branson, I mentioned to Donnabelle that I didn't have an ending for the story I had been writing about our friendship. I couldn't figure it out. Something was missing. Hers was the last to finish out of twenty-five stories. I thought a vacation from writing might prove helpful.

Our Branson trip included another Daniel O'Donnell concert. Because of a past experience, my husband had ordered tickets well in advance. Tour buses rolled in from all directions, which caused all of O'Donnell's shows to sell out. I wished Donnabelle could have been sitting there beside me, especially to hear his final song, "How Great Thou Art." His performance on stage and his interaction with fans off stage exposed his servant's heart.

For our last evening meal, my husband suggested a buffet-style restaurant with multiple food bars. That suited me fine. By the time we pulled into the parking lot, we assumed from the number of vehicles that we'd have quite a wait. Inside the door, people were standing in a roped-off section that looped back and forth several times before reaching the cashier.

Although I couldn't see the face of the person standing directly in front of me, I nudged my husband and quietly whispered that he could pass for Daniel O'Donnell's brother. When the man glanced my direction, his eyes gave away his identity. I felt my face begin to flush. Silently, my heart cried out in acknowledgment, *God, this is Your perfect timing!*

Mr. O'Donnell had not come to the restaurant alone. I also recognized Majella, his lovely and talented wife, but not the gentleman in his party. When they paused in conversation, I took the chance to speak with him. I consider the words we exchanged a gift from God.

Being respectful of his privacy in public, I tried to ignore his presence as we moved farther along in line. By the time we reached the last stretch of roped-off area, I felt pressured to heed a voice that was not audible except in my heart: *Time is running out. I placed you here for a reason. Continue talking.*

Not certain of what to say, I told Mr. O'Donnell about one of his greatest fans, Donnabelle. I said that I had written a story about her and others and explained the purpose for doing so. The words spoken from my heart perhaps touched his. In response, I felt a tender squeeze on my hand and heard the words, "God bless you."

Knowing our time in line together was about to end, I thanked him for our talk. I offered to send him a copy of my book of stories when published, acknowledging his busy schedule and the probability that he wouldn't have time to read it. He asked that it be mailed to Ireland and then asked my name. By the time I rested my head on a pillow that evening, I became aware that this *coincidental* meeting had given me the perfect ending for Donnabelle's story.

During the eight-hour trip home the following day, my husband and I listened to our newest CDs. His music blessed my soul with a new awareness of God. Although I didn't have another autographed book to give my friend, I had a godly experience to share that neither she nor I will ever forget.

Donnabelle and I thank God for uniting us in friendship with a purse and a prayer and for His many blessings.

Perhaps God gets my attention better when I'm standing in line. What better place is there to have a conversation? Whether I was standing in line behind Donnabelle or in line behind Mr. O'Donnell, God seemed to hold me captive, waiting for His plan to unfold.

Donnabelle and I, along with countless others throughout the world, continue to be inspired and uplifted by Daniel O'Donnell's singing. Although we don't know what lies ahead of us while living here on earth, we do know Who holds the future. Donnabelle and I thank God for uniting us in friendship with a purse and a prayer and for His many blessings.

Afterword

As I complete the last story, I find myself thinking about the first. I recall Genie standing in knee-high grass in his backyard, playing guitar and singing for me, an audience of one. Daniel O'Donnell, on the other hand, performed far from his homeland in a high-tech theater in front of thousands, accompanied by an orchestra, a band, and backup singers. A remarkable thought crosses my mind: Whether dressed in worn khaki pants or a lavish tuxedo, both sing for the same purpose, to glorify God.

My friends and I share these stories with you for the same reason—to give God the glory. "God has brought you out of darkness into his marvelous light. Now you must tell all the wonderful things he has done" (I Peter 2:9 CEV).

When I flip through the typed pages of stories from beginning to end, I wonder, *How, God, did all this happen?* I don't have an exact answer, but I do know this: If the Holy Spirit weren't real and active in everyday life, these pages would be blank.

On behalf of these people whose stories I've shared, I want to say thank you for opening your heart and reading the messages from ours. Instead of laying this book aside on a shelf, consider passing it on, in the hope that others may hear His call and respond, "That's You, God! I know That's You!"

ABOUT THE AUTHOR

Jane Perkins lives with her husband in a small town in western Kentucky, where she bases her ministry and writing. At the close of a teaching career in public schools, she felt called to devote herself to the writing of these true stories. Her son, John, now in his twenties, shares her love of photography and has collaborated with her in the compilation of her first book.

This collaboration continues in Perkins' second book, *A Mum and a Mission*, which she is writing from the perspective of an ongoing friendship of twenty-seven years with Genie Dickson, whose story is introduced in the first chapters of this book.